THE
DIANA COOPER
~ SCRAPBOOK ~

THE
DIANA COOPER
~ SCRAPBOOK ~

ARTEMIS COOPER

HAMISH HAMILTON·LONDON

DESIGN BY CRAIG DODD

ACKNOWLEDGEMENTS

All the photographs and cuttings are taken from Diana Cooper's family albums, and those by Cecil Beaton are reproduced by kind permission of Sotheby's Cecil Beaton Archive.

I would like to thank the following for their help in identifying people in the photographs: Susan Mary Alsop, who has also allowed me to quote from her book *To Marietta From Paris*; Alan Bell; Evangeline Bruce; Lord Charteris; the Duchess of Devonshire; Douglas Fairbanks Jr; David Herbert; Lady Katherine Giles; Mary Links; Martin Russell; and the Duke of Rutland.

I am particularly grateful to my father John Julius Norwich, my editor Christopher Sinclair-Stevenson, Hugo Vickers, and Philip Ziegler for all their help and suggestions on the text. Philip's biography *Diana Cooper* was invaluable, as was John Charmley's *Duff Cooper*, and this book is deeply indebted to their research. I would also like to thank my husband Antony Beevor: not only for all the work he has done on this book, but for his patience and unfailing humour.

My grandmother, Diana Cooper, who gave me more than I could ever thank her for, died last summer at the age of 93. I wish I could have put this book into her hands.

First published in Great Britain 1987
by Hamish Hamilton Ltd
27 Wrights Lane, London W8 5T7

Copyright © 1987 by Artemis Cooper

British Library Cataloguing in Publication Data

Cooper, Artemis
    Diana Cooper's scrapbook.
    1. Cooper, Diana, *1892-1986*   2. Great
    Britain—— Biography
    I. Title
    941.082′092′4   DA566.9.C638

ISBN 0-241-12133-7

Printed and bound in Great Britain
by Butler & Tanner Ltd, Frome and London

*Frontispiece: Diana dressed for
the Jewels of Empire Ball,
1926.*

CONTENTS

THE FAMILIES OF DUFF AND DIANA COOPER

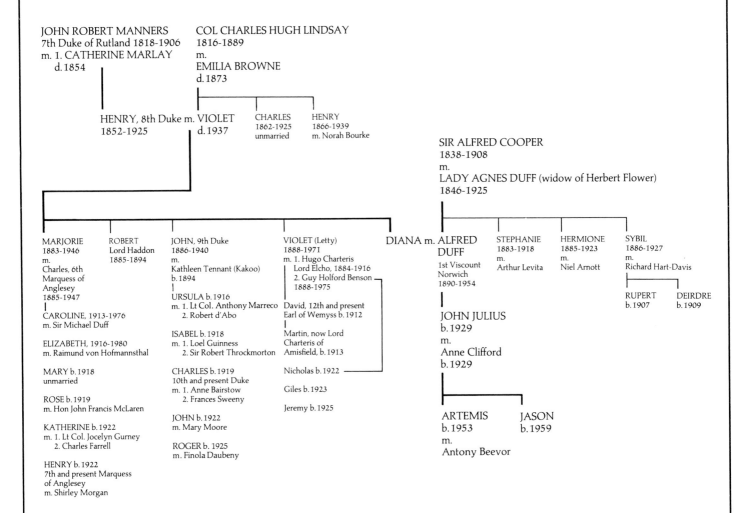

JOHN ROBERT MANNERS
7th Duke of Rutland 1818-1906
m. 1. CATHERINE MARLAY
    d. 1854

COL CHARLES HUGH LINDSAY
1816-1889
m.
EMILIA BROWNE
d. 1873

HENRY, 8th Duke m. VIOLET
1852-1925   d. 1937

CHARLES
1862-1925
unmarried

HENRY
1866-1939
m. Norah Bourke

SIR ALFRED COOPER
1838-1908
m.
LADY AGNES DUFF (widow of Herbert Flower)
1846-1925

MARJORIE
1883-1946
m.
Charles, 6th
Marquess of
Anglesey
1885-1947

CAROLINE, 1913-1976
m. Sir Michael Duff

ELIZABETH, 1916-1980
m. Raimund von Hofmannsthal

MARY b. 1918
unmarried

ROSE b. 1919
m. Hon John Francis McLaren

KATHERINE b. 1922
m. 1. Lt Col. Jocelyn Gurney
     2. Charles Farrell

HENRY b. 1922
7th and present Marquess
of Anglesey
m. Shirley Morgan

ROBERT
Lord Haddon
1885-1894

JOHN, 9th Duke
1886-1940
m.
Kathleen Tennant (Kakoo)
b. 1894

URSULA b. 1916
m. 1. Lt Col. Anthony Marreco
     2. Robert d'Abo

ISABEL b. 1918
m. 1. Loel Guinness
     2. Sir Robert Throckmorton

CHARLES b. 1919
10th and present Duke
m. 1. Anne Bairstow
     2. Frances Sweeny

JOHN b. 1922
m. Mary Moore

ROGER b. 1925
m. Finola Daubeny

VIOLET (Letty)
1888-1971
m. 1. Hugo Charteris
     Lord Elcho, 1884-1916
     2. Guy Holford Benson
     1888-1975

David, 12th and present
Earl of Wemyss b. 1912

Martin, now Lord
Charteris of
Amisfield, b. 1913

Nicholas b. 1922

Giles b. 1923

Jeremy b. 1925

DIANA m. ALFRED
DUFF

1st Viscount
Norwich
1890-1954

JOHN JULIUS
b. 1929
m.
Anne Clifford
b. 1929

ARTEMIS
b. 1953
m.
Antony Beevor

JASON
b. 1959

STEPHANIE
1883-1918
m.
Arthur Levita

HERMIONE
1885-1923
m.
Niel Arnott

SYBIL
1886-1927
m.
Richard Hart-Davis

RUPERT
b. 1907

DEIRDRE
b. 1909

INTRODUCTION

*H*ad he not been due to become Marquess of Granby, and then Duke of Rutland, Violet Lindsay would probably not have married Henry Manners. Charming and handsome, he was content with the duties and pleasures of an English gentleman, and seldom read anything more stimulating than a newspaper.

Violet, on the other hand, was passionate, intelligent, and an accomplished artist, whose exquisite pencil portraits were much prized by her friends. She had five children. The two eldest were Marjorie, later Marchioness of Anglesey, and Robert, Lord Haddon, who died at the age of nine. His marble monument at Haddon Hall is the most beautiful and moving work his mother ever created. Next came John, later the ninth Duke, who restored Haddon Hall to its former glory. Then came two daughters: Violet, known as Letty, who married Lord Elcho, the son of the Earl of Wemyss, and lastly Diana.

It is generally believed that Diana, born in 1892, was not the daughter of the Duke of Rutland but of Harry Cust, the greatest love of Violet's life. While still at Eton, his housemaster predicted that he was the boy of his generation most likely to become prime minister. However, his brilliance and his golden looks — which made him irresistible to women — took him no further than the editorship of the Pall Mall Gazette, and a short-lived career as an M.P. Both he and Violet were members of the Souls, the cultural wing of the British aristocracy. Its leading light was Arthur Balfour, and Diana's Soul pedigree was further embellished by having him as her godfather.

Until Henry Granby succeeded as Duke of Rutland and inherited Belvoir Castle, he and his family had lived quite modestly. The first few years of Diana's life were spent at Cockayne Hatley in Bedfordshire, a childhood Eden that was sold when she was six. She was shattered by its loss, which loomed large in her personal mythology, and put a horrible reality on Nanny's saying that 'things don't last for ever'. From Hatley they moved to No. 16 Arlington Street, which was to be the Rutlands' London house until 1925.

The theatrical grandeur of Belvoir was hard to take seriously — especially since the Duchess continued to act as though they had no money at all, at least for non-essentials. Despising food, she lived on a diet of Ovaltine and Marie biscuits. On a trip to Florence, she kept herself and the children on starvation rations, while arranging for the shipment of innumerable antique columns and marble statues back to Leicestershire.

In later years, it was hard to imagine Diana's sceptical view of her own beauty, but this and other quirks in her character can be traced back to her childhood. She was told by her mother that a slight bump on her forehead was the stump of a unicorn's horn. Then, at the age of ten, she contracted a type of infantile paralysis known as Erb's Disease. For weeks she had to lie in a darkened room, her life despaired of. The illness, and the special treatment received in the course of a long convalescence, encouraged her fears of abnormality. Physical self-confidence was not improved by the pronouncements of her aunts: a good child, but rather plain. There seemed no hope of the puppy-fat leaving that round, moon-like face.

Previous page: Diana aged eight by J. J. Shannon.

8

Above: Belvoir Castle in Leicestershire: rebuilt by James Wyatt on the orders of Elizabeth, 5th Duchess of Rutland, in 1816.

As with her ambivalent feelings about her looks (she once described herself as an anaemic blancmange), only close friends were aware that for all her high spirits, Diana was also prey to bouts of black melancholia. These moods, which she admitted were completely irrational, afflicted her throughout her life.

Among the contradictions in her character were a taste for adventure combined with a craving for security, and a combination of parsimony and extravagance inherited from her mother. Diana's compulsive dare-devilry was a determined attempt to overcome shyness. She dreaded the day when people would realise what she had always known — that she was not as pretty and amusing as they thought. Diana remembered that 'This lack of confidence and a hunted feeling of being discovered and exposed was certainly one of the shadows closing in.' It was this, together with her love of life, that made her push herself to the limit.

Diana often went to stay with the Beerbohm Trees near Brancaster. And it was here, aged thirteen, that she first discovered the pleasure of being admired by young men, for each summer a group of Oxford undergraduates, including her brother John, used to take a house for reading parties.

Their in-jokes, quick laughter, and conversation cross-fertilised by

different talents delighted Diana; and their pleasure in her company gave her a love of cliques that was to last all her life. She felt that everyone needed an audience to bring out the best in them, just as she did herself; and besides, *tête-à-têtes* alarmed her. She was afraid that her academic deficiencies might force the conversation to trail off into agonising silence. To avoid this humiliating possibility, she crammed herself with history, poetry, Shakespeare and Greek mythology — 'concealing the nine tenths of the iceberg of total ignorance', as she later described it.

By the age of sixteen, the looks for which she was to become famous were beginning to appear. Blonde hair and a luminous complexion enhanced the line of her face, which was becoming less round and more heart-shaped; and the gaze of her large pale blue eyes became startling. No longer treated as an honorary younger sister, she began to attract declarations of love; most of which were no more than extravagant fantasy, but none the less heady for that.

As well as arousing the ardent attentions of young men, she turned older heads. 'I think I must have been a snob in those days,' she wrote some fifty years later. 'All my loves were celebrities and generally very old ones. I must have been flirtatious too. I wanted passionately to be loved.'

When Diana came out in 1910, her beauty and vitality made her

Above: Haddon Hall in Derbyshire: the medieval and Tudor house abandoned by the Manners family for several centuries, lovingly restored by Diana's brother John, the 9th Duke.

Opposite: Diana, Irene Lawley, and Katherine Asquith.

presence a valuable asset to any party. With Oxford behind them, John's friends had taken up the life of fashionable London; and several of them became part of the inner circle that Diana called the Corrupt Coterie. Although the name would have been familiar to them, to what extent the members of the Coterie formed or felt themselves a cohesive group is debatable. Diana was the only one of them to write about them in this way. Her account came fifty years later, and was inevitably romanticised.

There was Patrick Shaw-Stewart, a Fellow of All Souls, who was to become the youngest director of Baring's Bank. Lord Ribblesdale's son Charles Lister, another intellectual, was a committed socialist. Edward Horner, although not nearly as brilliant, was tall, good looking and greatly valued for his charm and his amiable nature. Many people thought that he and Diana were secretly engaged. Alan Parsons, dark and slightly built, was quieter than the others, and married Diana's best friend, Viola Tree.

Another member of the Coterie was Duff Cooper. His father was a distinguished surgeon, Sir Alfred Cooper, who specialised in unmentionable complaints. His mother, Lady Agnes, was a sister of the Duke of Fife,

Left: Duff at his parents' house on the Isle of Arran.

though her progress through elopement and divorce meant that her family had long since cut her off. Sir Alfred was her third husband. Although Diana was wary of Duff's cynicism and amorous proclivities, she thoroughly enjoyed his mischievous humour and appetite for life.

The tragic death of Denis Anson marked, for Diana, the end of her hitherto carefree days. There was a party on board a pleasure boat on the Thames, and someone suggested swimming. Anson gave Diana his watch, and jumped in. He was drowned, as was one of the bandsmen who went to his rescue. Diana was deeply shaken and upset, and the publicity that followed was not kind.

It was not the first time, nor would it be the last, that the Coterie had attracted strong criticism. Patrick Shaw-Stewart had felt that they should increase their 'mutual admiration' to counter the opprobrium. Diana defined the relationship more clearly when she described their clique as 'very irritating to others and utterly satisfying and delightful to ourselves'.

With the exception of Julian Grenfell, the Coterie did not share in the national euphoria of August 1914. They tended to see the coming war as a tiresome interruption, while Diana strongly believed that the whole ghastly mess could be averted by some judicious string-pulling. But all her closest friends were soon in uniform save Alan Parsons, who was rejected on medical grounds, and Duff, who was kept back by the Foreign Office until 1917.

Diana signed on as a V.A.D. nurse at Guy's Hospital at the beginning of October, as part of the move to release trained nurses for Flanders. More than enough hardship followed, but a proud determination to see it through and to spite all the sceptics, from the Duchess to the popular press, kept her going.

The Duchess had vetoed her original plan of going to tend the soldiers in France, having been easily persuaded by Lady Dudley that her daughter would be raped on the spot. She was appalled by Diana's move to Guy's, for she maintained a typically aristocratic view of the nursing role appropriate to women of gentle birth. Diana's hospital work meant caring for the poor of the East End, and this lacked the romantic patriotism of soothing the brows of wounded subalterns. Diana was more vexed by the discipline that nurses were subjected to than the long hours of hard work. She was allowed no more than the odd couple of hours off to see her friends, some of them back on leave for only a few precious days.

This restriction alone was enough to persuade her to return home, when the Duchess decided to turn their house in Arlington Street into 'The Rutland Hospital for Officers'. The war allowed Diana far more freedom than an unmarried girl could normally have had, and her life became frenetic. However, she felt lonely with the Coterie split up. Duff was the only bachelor regularly on hand to chide her through moods of black despondency. His high spirits and reassuring presence began to present a serious attraction. This was inevitably accelerated after Raymond Asquith's death in 1916. Diana had been passionately drawn to Raymond, despite her friendship with his wife Katherine. He was the man she admired most in the world. Others stood no chance while he remained as yardstick.

Above and left: The drawing room at Gower Street, with painted piano and trompe l'oeil *panels by Rex Whistler.*

With his incorrigibly roving eye, Duff was not perhaps as besotted with Diana as some of his rivals; but he now began to lay serious siege to her affections. Diana never guessed how much he meant to her until he was released by the Foreign Office to join the Grenadier Guards. His self-indulgence, particularly his drinking and gambling, caused her to despair — mainly because they seemed detrimental to the ambition she so admired. But with Duff's battalion preparing for France in that spring of 1918, the time of Ludendorff's great offensive, the dangers awaiting him silenced all reproof.

Duff's luck held. As a result of one memorable attack, his bravery and competence won him the D.S.O., a rare honour for a junior officer. In a correspondence of mounting emotion, he and Diana became secretly engaged. Together they made ambitious plans for the future, and plotted how to obtain the Rutlands' blessing on their marriage.

The Duchess's opposition turned out even worse than they had feared. After dreams of a brilliant match for her most beautiful daughter, the thought of Diana wasting herself on an impecunious Foreign Office clerk, with no prospects and a reputation for dissolute living, sent her into a mortified rage. The situation was made worse by the fact that Diana could not bring herself to tell her mother that she loved him. 'I should have told her I was desperately in love,' Diana realised later, 'and thrown myself sobbing on her mercy. Instead some silly pride forbade me to admit that I loved Duff.'

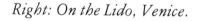

Right: On the Lido, Venice.

It was not the first time that Diana's diffidence had created misunderstandings. Half-afraid of passion, her reserve had provoked accusations of coldness from frustrated lovers in the Coterie, who could not believe in her insistence on keeping her virginity, when all around were losing theirs. Eventually, helped by the Duke's indulgence, the Duchess came to relent; Diana and Duff only had to wait six months before they were married at St Margaret's, Westminster, in June 1919.

After a honeymoon in Italy, Duff and Diana returned to London and their precarious finances. Duff's salary at the Foreign Office was £350 a year, and it was only thanks to an allowance from his mother that they stood a chance of making ends meet. The Rutlands, although they had accepted their new son-in-law, did not increase Diana's allowance. The lavish presents displayed at the wedding, from royalty and other grand friends, can only have emphasised the relative poverty of the couple.

It was not long before disaster struck. Diana, who was watching the Armistice Day fireworks from a rooftop, took a step backwards to get a better view. The result was that she crashed through a skylight, breaking her leg and hip. For six weeks she lay in the drawing room of her hosts Norman and Marion Holden, with her leg in traction. Here she was visited by a constant stream of admirers who surrounded her with flowers, and this impromptu salon led to D. H. Lawrence's portrait of her in his novel *Aaron's Rod*, as Lady Artemis Hooper.

After a period of house-hunting in a wheel-chair pushed by Duff, they moved into No. 90 Gower Street. Bloomsbury was not a fashionable area, ('What a quarter, Violet, what a quarter!' Lady Scarbrough exclaimed to Diana's mother, hands raised in horror), but the house was seldom short of visitors. With financial help and advice from the Duchess, and relying always on her friends, Diana soon had the house she wanted for entertaining. The parties became famous. Rubinstein played the piano, Hilaire Belloc recited verses, or Chaliapin sang, while Lord Beaverbrook supplied the drink.

Duff, although undoubtedly able, did not enjoy the whole-hearted admiration of his superiors. When Lord Curzon read in a gossip column that the Duff Coopers were thinking of buying the piano nobile of the Palazzo Labia in Venice, he complained that Duff was getting too much leave. Duff proved this to be untrue; but Curzon was convinced that Duff's work suffered from his fondness for 'social relaxation'. (They never did live in the Palazzo Labia, but many years later it was the scene of Diana's triumph as the Tiepolo Cleopatra, at the Beistegui ball.)

Certainly Duff had very little taste for administrative detail, preferring whenever possible to leave it to subordinates. However, in 1922 he became Private Secretary to the Parliamentary Under Secretary at the Foreign Office: a job reserved for the most promising young men. Professional contact with the world of politics, his friendship with Winston Churchill, and the encouragement of Sir Robert Vansittart fired Duff's ambition to enter Parliament. But however great his enthusiasm or commitment, he never lost a fastidious, eighteenth-century cynicism towards public life.

Above: Diana and Max Reinhardt at Leopoldskron, during her audition for 'The Miracle', 1923.

Duff's attitude to marriage also belonged to the Age of Enlightenment, or rather the Regency. It owed nothing to Victorian values. He believed in discretion, but loathed hypocrisy. Diana shared his views, and a pattern of mutual tolerance was established: Duff of Diana's friends, a number of whom he heartily disliked, and Diana of Duff's mistresses. At times Diana had to fight hard to control her jealousy, but it was remarkable how many became her friends. Wallis Simpson was to remark that the worst thing about an affair with Duff would be having Diana round to comfort you as soon as it was over. Although one might think their tacit pact was one-sided, Diana did not see it that way, since friendship was far more important to her than sexual love. But whatever the ingredients, the extraordinary success of their marriage is undeniable.

If anything shadowed those early years, it was financial worry. Diana was utterly committed to 'The Plan' to get Duff out of the Foreign Office and on the road to a glittering future. And because it needed a lot more capital than they could raise by conventional means, she was ready to seize almost any opportunity to earn money. Some of her projects backfired, but others worked, like articles for society pages written by Duff and signed by Diana.

The key to 'The Plan''s success proved to be her beauty and dramatic talent. Diana's first big chance, an offer of $75,000 from the great silent movie director D. W. Griffith, was thwarted first by her forthcoming marriage, and then by her accident. Another soon came her way, although the director concerned — J. Stewart Blackton — was a hack compared to Griffith. Diana's mother had at first been terrified that Diana would become *déclassée* by such a profession. But the enormous fee, and the fact that her performance was widely applauded, more than calmed family scruples.

Whatever the defects of her two films — Diana described *The Virgin Queen* as 'an inartistic lark' — they brought her to the attention of Max Reinhardt, the greatest impresario of the age. In the summer of 1923, he invited her to come to Salzburg and audition for the role of the Madonna in his revival of a medieval mystery play called *The Miracle*, which was scheduled to open in New York that winter. To her enormous surprise and even greater trepidation, she got the part.

Duff and Diana sailed to America in November 1923. They were lodged in a suite in the Ambassador Hotel, while Diana's maid, Miss Wade, was alarmed to discover that her room was on the eighteenth floor. Duff was very grateful for Cole Porter's present of a case of Bourbon and a case of Scotch, but found Prohibition hard to get used to. He nearly collapsed when the waiter asked if he would have tea or coffee with his lunch.

He stayed a fortnight with Diana before returning to London in early December. Without his reassuring presence, she became a prey to constant fears and apprehensions. But once the agonies of dress rehearsals and the first night were over, Diana settled into the demanding routine that was expected of her, as the star of a magnificent production.

Though Reinhardt had staked everything on *The Miracle*, it was a greater success than he had dared to hope. For the next four years the production went on tour, each stage being planned like a military campaign. An army of carpenters and electricians arrived in advance of the actors, in order to turn the auditorium of the largest theatre in town into a medieval cathedral. The local press was buzzing with anticipation by the time the cast of three hundred arrived by train, two weeks later. Diana was invariably met with bouquets, photographers and journalists. From the station she was swept into a luxurious and usually complimentary suite in a grand hotel. As the beautiful daughter of a real English Duke, the press could not have enough of her. Whatever she said was news.

After a few days of rehearsal came the excitement of the opening night. Today, *The Miracle* would be greeted with far more scepticism than it was in America in the 1920s. Yet for people who had never seen a cathedral, the set alone was breath-taking. What followed was not simply a mystery play but a powerful psychological drama, which left the majority of its audience emotionally drained and spiritually uplifted.

Diana's schedule was exhausting. As well as rehearsals that went on well into the early hours, the *Miracle* publicity machine filled her days with interviews and women's lunches, and engagements to open bazaars and attend civic receptions. She was besieged by admirers, who sent her presents and begged for the honour of taking her to dinner. And yet, despite her busy life and all the adulation she received, Diana missed Duff cruelly. She described her letters to him at this time as 'an unpardonable Jeremiad, a daily Gummidge-whine'.

Every penny was being saved to get Duff into Parliament. Diana's family tried to secure their local borough of Melton Mowbray for him, but were unsuccessful. Duff himself described his views as reactionary, and feared

that they might find no place in modern politics. But in July 1924, when Ramsay MacDonald's first Labour Government was already showing signs of stress, he was accepted as Conservative candidate for Oldham, a seat formerly held by Winston Churchill.

His first taste of electioneering began in October. He was grateful to Diana's sisters, Letty and Marjorie, who helped canvass — but it was not until Diana arrived, released from *The Miracle* for the election, that his campaign took off. Although he could speak with energy and conviction, Duff was shy with people outside his own social class. Diana's fame, combined with her warm spontaneity, made her immediately popular — though she was terrified of doing or saying something that might wreck Duff's chances. A graver danger was that the attention surrounding Diana might eclipse the candidate.

The first time she heard him speak in public, Diana was amazed by Duff's proficiency. Even in his later career, when he had to deliver the Army Estimates, he never used notes while making a speech.

> The sensible sentences rolled out without hesitation. There was nothing flustered about his calm stance and clear delivery, his hands clasping the lapels of his coat in a classical nineteenth-century way.

When he won the election by several thousand votes, Diana's pride was overwhelming. Her choice of a husband had been vindicated, and she noted with satisfaction that her family saw Duff as the young Disraeli.

It was a great advantage to ride into politics on the crest of a Bolshevik scare prompted by the Zinoviev letter. (Only much later was this found to be a Secret Service forgery.) But Duff, who had hammered away with the anti-Communist rhetoric of that election, soon proved himself an impressive and remarkably liberal member of his party. A strong supporter of the League of Nations, his stand on foreign issues was humane and democratic; and at home, during the General Strike, he argued for conciliation with the unions.

Duff's maiden speech, delivered on December 15, was widely hailed as brilliant. His only regret was that Diana was not there to share his triumph, since she had had to return to *The Miracle* shortly after his election. Without her help, his entry into Parliament might have taken much longer, but having such a wife brought disadvantages as well. Her irresistible urge to pull strings on his behalf was to cause him some embarrassment in the course of his career; and her butterfly image, however undeserved, hardly helped a husband whom many tended to see as insufficiently serious.

It would be equally wrong to blame Diana for Duff's failure to fulfil the predictions that he would one day be prime minister, or at least foreign secretary. Duff was capable of intense work when interested; but unlike that rumbustious fighter Churchill, who lived and breathed politics, he took pride in having a full life outside Parliament. He visited his constituency no more than necessary, and infinitely preferred the bar at White's to hanging around the House of Commons. Political theory, by-laws and local issues were grey and tedious, compared to good conversation and impromptu couplets.

SPOKE WITHOUT NOTES

It is unusual in these days to see M.P.'s observing the old Parliamentary rule of speaking without notes.

This feat was performed by Mr. Duff Cooper, the Financial Secretary to the War Office, in introducing the Army Estimates last night.

Above: A cartoon of Duff, 1935.

Opposite: Diana as the Madonna, in one of the first photographs of her by Cecil Beaton.

Economical by nature, Diana saved all she could of her American earnings — though there were the occasional splashes, like buying her mother a car, and herself a fur coat of summer ermine. She also commissioned Rex Whistler to paint a series of *trompe l'oeil* panels for the Gower Street drawing room. But Duff's passion for gambling, good wine, pretty women and first editions continued to outstrip his resources. His artless complaint at how disheartening it was to find himself overdrawn when he had indulged in no extravagances, prompted reproofs from Diana that were more anxious than angry.

The continuing success of *The Miracle* occupied half of each year for four years, and took her across the United States. In 1925, Diana's old friend Iris Tree — 'that dearest romantic in clown's clothes' — was signed up to play the Nun opposite Diana's Madonna. Life on tour was no longer a drudgery, and when Hugo von Hofmannsthal's son Raimund joined the company the following year, it became even more enjoyable. In Hollywood, people said that Diana should consider doing more films. But a visit to Marion Davies in the Metro-Goldwyn studios brought back the 'grisly' light of the studio, and 'the snail's pace that outwears any patience', and quickly stifled any temptation she may have had in that direction.

Reinhardt took *The Miracle* to Dortmund in 1928. Rosamund Pinchot, who was to have played the Nun, broke her ankle at the last moment. There were no understudies; and Diana had to take on both parts, twice a day, for a week. Before each performance a doctor came and injected her with 'a glass-full of camphor' to give her strength. Whether or not this eased the strain on her health, she was obliged to take a fortnight's rest in London. She was not well as the show continued through Prague, Budapest and Vienna.

This ordeal marked the end of Diana's *Miracle* days for the time being, and that winter she accepted an invitation from Sidney Herbert to join him on holiday in the Bahamas. Since Diana and Duff had been apart for Christmas for the last five years, and she was very half-hearted about the trip, it was strange that she should go. Loyalty to Sidney Herbert was one reason; but the years of travel had become a habit, and she was restless.

Once in Nassau, she began to feel distinctly unwell. She came to the conclusion she was pregnant, and could not decide whether she was thrilled or horrified by the fact. She had always been ambivalent about children. 'Indeed', she wrote,

> I had made the best of my barrenness and persuaded myself that children were sharper than serpents' teeth. Girls were sure to be plain and without virtue, boys dishonest, even queer, and certainly gambling drunkards.

Nevertheless, in the course of nine years of marriage, she had consulted endless fertility specialists and underwent an operation to enable her to have children. Now the great moment had arrived, she panicked and took a dose of quinine to bring on an abortion — and was deeply relieved when nothing happened.

John Julius, Duff and Diana's only son, was born in London on September 15, 1929, after a difficult birth that involved a caesarian section;

The TATLER

Vol. CXIX. No. 1551. London, March 18, 1931 POSTAGE: Inland 2d.; Canada and Newfoundland, 1½d.; Foreign, 4d. Price One Shilling

Speaight: New Bond Street

LADY DIANA COOPER AND HER SON JOHN

Whatever opinions, and there are many, are held with regard to the "needle" fight taking place in that stronghold of Conservatism, St. George's, all parties are agreed that Lady Diana Cooper is a charming and potent factor in the struggle. A constituency full of young servants, undoubtedly readers of those powerful organs owned by the newspaper Lords, may use the flapper vote presented them by Mr. Baldwin to his undoing. On the other hand, the violence of the attack may bring about a revulsion of feeling in his favour. In any case we are able to publish here a very attractive side-light on the battle

c

a fact commemorated in the latter half of his name. He learnt to read early, and his mother took his education very seriously.

Lines must be drawn three quarters of an inch apart for his writing and he must be given funny sentences that amuse him to write. He must practise the piano regularly with scales and five-finger exercises, and learn by heart.

Luckily John Julius enjoyed his lessons, and was blessed with an engagingly easy disposition. While still very small, his monthly nurse had exclaimed 'Poor baby — he's only trying to please!' Diana adored him, but until he grew a little older, she was always relieved to hand him back to Nanny. Friendships and Duff's career remained the most absorbing interests.

Duff was a romantic Tory. He shared the 'One Nation' views of young colleagues such as Anthony Eden and Harold Macmillan, who like him had seen front line service and retained a sense of obligation towards the soldiers they had commanded. They felt little in common with those in the Party usually described as 'the hard-faced men who had done well out of the war'. Under Stanley Baldwin, the archetypal decent Englishman, Duff's career flourished. In 1928 he became Financial Secretary at the War Office. But at the general election in the following year the tide swung against the Conservatives, and he lost Oldham in spite of strenuous efforts. (Diana too did her best in this election, but being heavily pregnant she could not repeat her 'knock-about turn' that had been such a success in 1924.)

Ramsay MacDonald's Labour Government took office for the second time. In 1930, Baldwin faced the determined efforts of the press barons, Beaverbrook and Rothermere, to unseat him from the Party leadership with their creation — the Empire Free Trade movement. His agreement with Socialist policy on allowing India Dominion status had brought furious attacks from the right of the Party and Winston Churchill.

When the normally safe seat of St George's Westminster became vacant in late 1930, the impending by-election was quickly turned into a proposed vote of no confidence by Baldwin's opponents. Duff volunteered to fight the seat as Baldwin's champion, a move which many considered rash when taking into account the power of the popular press. But Duff, backed to the hilt by Baldwin, fought a very effective battle by concentrating his onslaught on the arrogance of the 'Yellow Press' in trying to change the Conservative Party's leadership. This was the issue which prompted Baldwin's famous phrase about its desire for 'power without responsibility — the prerogative of the harlot through the ages'.

Diana and her family fought hard on Duff's behalf. She herself was lent a car by Lord Ashfield, the founder of London Transport. It arrived every morning with a chauffeur, and a fresh white gardenia. Duff won the election so convincingly that the anti-Baldwin campaign collapsed and Beaverbrook sued for peace. Acclaimed by Baldwin, Chamberlain and the rest of the Party leadership, Duff returned to Parliament in the spring of 1931, with the virtual certainty of office the moment Baldwin returned to power.

That August, the sterling crisis and a split in the Labour Party led to the formation of the National Government. And Baldwin, despite the scramble for places in the coalition, returned Duff to the War Office, this time as Under-Secretary.

With Duff securely back in office and in a role that was not very demanding, he and Diana were able to spend much more time in Sussex. West House, Aldwick, was a small late eighteenth-century farmhouse near Bognor, which had been given to Violet Rutland by her admirer, the Duke of Portland; and she in turn had given it to Diana. Duff loved the place as much as Diana did, and it was here that he wrote his first book, *Talleyrand*, published in 1932. It received considerable praise and attention, and sold well.

Diana, who always expected the worst, had been terrified that it might be met with indifference or even hostility. She was overjoyed at his success, one consequence of which was a request to write the official biography of

Field Marshal Earl Haig. Duff overruled his own misgivings, and accepted Lady Haig's commission. Although the considerable advance removed financial worries, it was a decision he later regretted — for the difficulties in obtaining access to the material, the time involved, and the compromises he found himself having to make. The critics dealt harshly with the book, but there was a word of consolation from Margot Asquith: her auto-biography had been just as cruelly received, she told Duff; but on re-reading it recently, she had found it excellent.

Over the course of the St George's by-election, Diana was put in a curious position: a man who had been devoted to her for years was fighting a savage battle with her beloved Duff. When Diana came to see Max Beaverbrook in his office, to beg him to temper his newspaper's attacks on her husband, he agreed to help. Duff, usually mortified by his wife's inter-vention, must have been grateful on this occasion. Without it, the *Daily Express* campaign would have been a good deal more unpleasant.

Duff had always disliked Max Beaverbrook; not from jealousy, but distaste for the coarse and ruthless energy that drove him. Diana, who liked powerful people and the glittering gifts they showered on her, was genu-inely fond of her 'demon friend', and had made him John Julius's god-father. Her natural instinct was to defend her friends stoutly, which the present situation forbade. To find that the political battle had not changed Beaverbrook's affection for her was therefore a great relief.

Once the excitement of the by-election was over and Duff safely seated in Parliament again, Diana looked about for new ways to employ her time. Since she was not the ideal committee person, her good works were largely confined to writing begging letters on behalf of various charities to her rich friends. She augmented the family income by advertising certain products, and there was the occasional job of public relations. When she suggested reviving *The Miracle*, everybody thought she was mad; but she persevered, arguing that since it had had a great success in England before the Great War, why not now? C. B. Cochran, who had put together the original pro-duction in 1912, thought it was worth trying again. In the spring *The Miracle* reappeared, with Diana as the Madonna and Tilly Losch as the Nun. It was not as lavish as Reinhardt's version, and British audiences were not as ecstatic as the American ones had been; but it was a success, and ran for many months.

'THE MADONNA' DIANA MANNERS

Two years before, Diana had received a letter from Cecil Beaton, asking if he could photograph her. She was pregnant at the time, and had written back, 'Please ask me again after the ordeal.' The photographs of Diana as the Madonna in the London production were the first he took of her, and many more followed as their friendship ripened over the years.

The Miracle went on tour of England, Wales, and Scotland, and it was during this time that Diana met Evelyn Waugh, in the course of a cross-country treasure hunt. In his biography of the novelist, Christopher Sykes remembers the evening vividly: the three of them dined together at a pub at Bray, where Evelyn kept the whole table in fits of laughter with his impressions of Emerald Cunard.

Diana appears in his novels as Mrs Algernon Stitch; first in *Scoop*, and

later in *The Sword of Honour* trilogy. His description of Julia Stitch's morning was typical of the way Diana started most days. She woke early, and breakfasted on a glass of tea with lemon, heavily sweetened with saccharine. Her correspondence and the business of the day were all done in bed, while friends dropped in and the telephone rang incessantly till noon. Bathing, making-up and dressing were crammed into ten minutes; then she was off in her car, rushing from one appointment to another.

Duff and Diana were frequently seen in the company of the Prince of Wales, who was determined to give the monarchy a tone of stylish informality. The pattern of weekends at Fort Belvedere hardly changed when he became King in 1936. Diana described the house as a toy fortress with magnificent views. The guests enjoyed every comfort, and life revolved around the golf course, the swimming pool, and cocktails shaken by the

monarch himself. That summer, Duff and Diana were invited to join him and Mrs Simpson for a cruise on the yacht *Nahlin*.

The cruise was regarded as a scandal; and when it became evident that the King had decided to marry Mrs Simpson, whatever the cost, his previous popularity was seriously damaged. Duff, who was summoned for advice, urged him to think again, saying that public opinion would never forgive Wallis if he abandoned the throne. After the abdication in December, Duff and Diana resigned themselves to the fact that they would probably not be so popular with the new, more sober court of George VI. But four months later they were invited to Windsor Castle, where they instinctively liked King George and his Queen — for whom Diana held a deep and admiring affection for the rest of her life. Comparing Fort Belvedere to Windsor, Diana told Chips Channon: 'That was an operetta, this is an institution.'

The Duchess of Rutland, who had been ill for some time, died just before Christmas 1937. Although Diana's relationship with her mother had been stormy before her marriage, it had steadily improved ever since. As John Julius grew up, Diana often sought her mother's advice on his toys, clothes, and — most importantly — his education. Diana mourned her death bitterly. The Duchess had spent her last years doing up a magnificent house in Chapel Street, which she left to her youngest daughter; and the house in Gower Street, which held some of Diana's happiest memories, was sold some months later.

Duff, who had watched the ominous rise of Germany with more suspicion than most, became seriously concerned for the future of Europe. In the summer of 1933, on their way to join Chips Channon in Austria, he and Diana had stopped in Bavaria and stayed by chance in the same hotel as Hitler. There, they witnessed preparations for the first great Nuremberg rally. Duff had disliked Germany ever since studying the language there in 1913, for the Foreign Office examination. Twenty years later the vision of the same country, once again 'preparing for war on a scale and with an enthusiasm that are astounding and terrible', made a deep impression. He was one of the first to influence Churchill and to speak out strongly about the danger, in spite of the hostility it aroused in his own party, and the Beaverbrook and Rothermere press.

In June 1934, Duff's transfer to the Treasury as Financial Secretary had put him under Neville Chamberlain: a Chancellor of the Exchequer who began by warning him not to speak out on Germany. Chamberlain nevertheless praised his work, and following the successful general election of November 1935 Duff was asked to join the Cabinet as Secretary of State for War.

Duff's continued preoccupation with the Nazi threat, both in Cabinet defending the Army Estimates against Chamberlain's cuts, and outside in public speeches, made him many enemies and irked Chamberlain in particular. It was therefore a surprise, not least to Duff, when following Baldwin's retirement in the early summer of 1937 he was not dismissed but promoted to First Lord of the Admiralty. Whether or not Chamberlain's motives were to prevent him attacking the government's defence and foreign policy from the back benches, his promotion was a great relief. Duff, although beginning to feel disenchanted with politics, did not want his career to end just yet.

Diana was even more delighted, and began to redecorate Admiralty House with great enthusiasm. Soon the place was awash with mermaids, tritons, dolphins, shells, anchors, paintings of naval battles, busts of Nelson, and sea-blue silk held back with golden ropes. The greatest perk however, was the First Lord's official yacht, *HMS Enchantress*.

In the following year, 1938, it was not only the European situation which began to look black. Duff's position in the government appeared depressingly precarious. Impervious to argument, Chamberlain flatly rejected any attempt to improve the country's defences. It might seem surprising that Duff made little attempt to support Anthony Eden in February 1938, when Chamberlain's private dealings with Mussolini forced his Foreign Secretary's resignation. But Duff did not regard the Italian dictator as a serious threat, and above all, he saw little reason to stick his neck out for a colleague who apparently vilified him. Duff never discovered why Eden disliked him so much, but this antipathy continued to sour their relations and Duff's career during the war to come.

In March the Nazis took over Austria. Duff, who was ill at the time,

Right: Duff as First Lord of the Admiralty, inspecting a naval guard of honour.

immediately wrote to Chamberlain urging an immediate increase in the Navy Estimates as a warning to Berlin, but achieved nothing. His strong recommendation to support France in its treaty obligations towards Czechoslovakia fared no better. Duff the Francophile was out of step with his fellow Tories and the service chiefs, who tended to dislike and distrust their ally.

In August 1938 the First Lord of the Admiralty and his wife, accompanied by Brendan Bracken and Diana's niece Elizabeth Paget, sailed to the Baltic on *HMS Enchantress* for a round of official visits. In Kiel Duff, to his disgust, had to propose a toast to Hitler. At Gdynia he had long talks with the Polish foreign minister Colonel Beck, who kept reiterating Poland's determination to resist Germany. Later, Diana found herself having to resist Beck's advances in a night club. In Danzig however, she fell for the League of Nations Commissioner, Carl Burckhardt. This 'glorious Swiss' had been a great friend of Hugo von Hofmannsthal, and Diana found his intellectual conversation rather daunting. But after Duff and Raymond Asquith, Carl Burckhardt was to become her most passionate attachment. He came into her life at a good time, for she had been feeling her age.

As a very young man, Raimund von Hofmannsthal had loved her. Now, with a brief and unhappy marriage to Alice Astor behind him, he was wooing Liz Paget. Liz's parents Charles and Marjorie Anglesey were not happy about this romance, and had sent their daughter on the *Enchantress* cruise to get her away from Raimund. But, wherever the ship docked, a bouquet of orchids was waiting for her, and a year later they were married.

After their next two ports of call — Helsingfors, now Helsinki, where they entertained Marshal Mannerheim on board, and Stockholm — the

Enchantress suddenly had to leave Copenhagen under full steam for England. The concentration of German troops on the Czech frontier had prompted an emergency Cabinet meeting in London.

It has often been said that the Munich crisis was one of Duff's finest hours. He never concealed his reluctance to leave the Admiralty — both because he felt it better to stay where he might still have some influence on events, and also because he was frankly loath to give up a position he enjoyed and a salary he needed. But having forced Chamberlain to let him mobilise the Fleet as proof of British resolve, and having then found that the Prime Minister had still given Hitler everything he wanted, the decision was made. He could stomach neither the sophistry of Chamberlain's justification nor the dishonour to Britain, and resigned. Diana was predictably desolated at the loss for both of them as she supervised the packing up at Admiralty House. But the inundation of congratulatory mail, more than four thousand letters from all over the world, was enough to confirm her great pride in Duff's action.

Once the heat of the moment was passed and the move to Chapel Street over, they both felt drained and dejected. At least a handsome contract for a weekly article in the *Evening Standard* averted a financial crisis. Duff was nevertheless unable to use this platform to air his views forcefully. Chamberlain's control over the Party was absolute. And Duff found himself being warned by his constituency association that he would not be their candidate at the next election if he further criticised the Government.

Duff urged Diana to get away to lift her spirits. It was often the most effective cure for her black moods, and in the early spring of 1939 she took John Julius skiing. At the Italian frontier she seized the opportunity to point out to him the idiocy of the bannered slogan, 'Mussolini is always right!' In April she and Duff went to Paris and in June she went back to Geneva to see Carl Burckhardt.

August was spent at Bognor in a mood of farewell to rural peace. Diana could not help thinking of that other summer exactly a quarter of a century before, when her world had been oblivious of the horrors ahead. This time they were only too aware, but that seemed cold comfort. On the sea front at Bognor, buying lobsters and prawns with John Julius on the morning of September 1, she heard the announcement of Hitler's invasion of Poland. Diana sank into a resigned despair.

Duff, to his dismay, found employment in any government capacity barred to him. Chamberlain was unforgiving. Even Winston Churchill, brought in as First Lord of the Admiralty, could not prevail. It must have struck Duff as a harsh irony that just under a year after he had forced Chamberlain to let him mobilise the Fleet, all to no avail, Churchill should now become the hero of the hour by giving the same order prematurely.

Diana wept at the pathos of seeing Duff go off to report for duty with the Grenadiers, in his old-fashioned ensign's uniform and puttees. But he was forced to admit that a lieutenant of nearly fifty, whom generals still called 'Sir' because he had been Minister of War, was more of an embarrassment than a help.

With nothing useful to do in London, Duff decided to go ahead with a

Above: Duff and Diana at Bognor in the summer of 1939, with Noel in the back.

previously planned lecture tour in the United States. At least there, he reasoned, some good could be done in a propaganda role. On October 12 they sailed from Southampton. To begin with the trip did little to lift Diana's gloomy unease. She felt disoriented in New York. It was no longer recognisable as the city which had worshipped her during *The Miracle*, but far more disheartening was the general indifference to the fate of Europe. She did not enjoy the parties and her nervousness made her ill. But their unexpectedly warm reception in Washington, particularly at the White House, restored Diana's confidence. Roosevelt remembered her from the Paris Peace Conference of 1919 and expressed his admiration for Duff's stand in 1938. Later, he arranged for Duff to return for private talks. The trip had been worthwhile after all, and that, Diana felt, would spite those in England who criticised Duff for making money in America while his country was in danger.

After the success in Washington, Diana was back on form making every party go well, even the often sticky after-lecture dinners where she made up for Duff's prickly shyness. The high point of their tour was staying in Hollywood with Jack Warner. Diana had been very reluctant at first. 'I had fought it, fearing the high standard of clothes and up-to-the-markishness. Duff, on the other hand was yearning for the stars.' Far from feeling 'an undesirable alien' as she had feared, Diana was thrilled at their reception and firmly applauded Elsa Maxwell's violent denunciation of a Nazi sympathiser. In New York she visited Iris who was living in an 'underground room that is 50% charm and the other 50% Zola' and, with Duff 'packed off to a smart dinner', the two women dined riotously in an Armenian restaurant.

When Duff and Diana returned to England in March 1940 Churchill, who succeeded Chamberlain after the invasion of Norway, kept his promise that Duff should have a part in his government by making him

Left: Diana and John Julius in a silhouette by Baroness von Meydel.

Minister of Information. Duff's contacts in Fleet Street, plus a talent for sound argument and rousing speeches, seemed excellent qualifications for the post. But it was soon obvious that the new ministry had no effective power. This, combined with Duff's instinctive distaste for censorship and propaganda, and an inability to flatter and cajole the press into accepting them, made his time as Minister very unhappy.

During those days following the end of the phoney war, the country braced itself for invasion. Signposts were taken down, shotguns and opera glasses donated to the Home Guard, and Diana dashed around trying to save anti-Nazi Germans from internment, giving blood and working at the YMCA canteen. She rose at 6.30 to join the team preparing breakfast for four hundred air raid wardens, washed up till noon, then returned to Chapel Street for an afternoon of packing up their possessions for storage at Belvoir. There was still time to see people, especially those off to fight. 'Evelyn Waugh,' she observed, 'now an officer in the Marines with as smart a little moustache as Errol Flynn, has never been so happy.' They also had dinner with Winston Churchill at Admiralty House, where a pallet bed had replaced Diana's extravaganza of gold tridents and dolphins.

Above right: John Julius at the Preparatory School of Upper Canada College, Toronto.

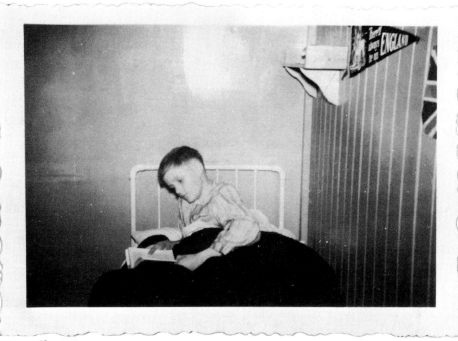

Duff's job was not made any easier when Diana leapt at the American Ambassador's suggestion that John Julius should be included among the child evacuees going to the United States. The fact that the 'Minister of Morale' was packing his son off to America while urging the rest of the country to man the barricades caused a great deal of criticism.

Once Chapel Street was locked up, Duff and Diana moved into a suite on the eighth floor of the Dorchester Hotel with only the minimum of possessions. Diana enjoyed the feeling of camping out in grandeur, and the hotel was full of friends. These included Ann O'Neill (later to marry Lord Rothermere and Ian Fleming), Pamela Berry, Virginia Cowles, and Emerald Cunard, who had a suite on the floor below. Diana described the Dorchester's restaurant as 'reminiscent of *S.S. Titanic*, jam-packed now with passengers and crew that one knows too well'.

Although country-house weekends continued, Diana grew progressively more afraid of London during the Blitz — especially since Duff refused to share her apprehensions, and preferred to sleep peacefully through the raids rather than scuttle down to an overcrowded basement. When she could no longer bear the bombs, Diana retired to Bognor. There, she decided she could best help the war effort by becoming a smallholder — 'Dig for Victory' was a slogan which appealed to her — and she called on her great friend Conrad Russell for advice.

Conrad Russell was a gentle, scholarly farmer who had become Diana's devoted admirer during *The Miracle*'s tour of Wales. At her request, he came to help set up the small farm, which was to become the rural idyll of Diana's life. Her success surprised her almost as much as her friends, who came to stay and were roped in to help with the chores. Daisy Fellowes rented Chapel Street, and Duff kept a room there — but he spent most nights at Bognor, and commuted to London.

In June, Duff made one last attempt to gain more power for the Ministry of Information, but without success. Perhaps this unrelieved frustration was partly to blame for the decision he took the following month, and for which his term as Minister is often remembered. William Connor, 'Cassandra' of the *Daily Mirror*, had written a venomous attack on P. G. Wodehouse and the latter's broadcasts from Berlin. The BBC refused to accept it unless it was toned down. When Duff heard about this he was furious, and instructed the BBC to put it out uncut. It was a sad ending to a sad period of his life.

At the end of July 1941, Duff handed over the Ministry of Information to Brendan Bracken, and was appointed Chancellor of the Duchy of Lancaster. Churchill then sent him to Singapore, to review the situation in the Far East. He and Diana arrived there in mid-September. His report — which said that unless Britain strengthened and speedily reorganised both the civil and military administration, it would lose control of the area — was in London at the end of October. There was no response from the Cabinet for a month, and by then it was already too late. In early December the Japanese invaded Malaya.

Duff was told to remain where he was, form a war council, and give political guidance. But once again he had no real power, and his presence was deeply resented by both the Governor and the Commander-in-Chief. In February 1942, when the situation was obviously irretrievable, he was instructed to return to England. Inevitably, but unfairly as Churchill recognised, Duff's political career suffered from this association with the greatest military disaster of the war.

Diana resumed her life at Bognor, with 'the dung and swill, curds and whey and spiders'. Another smallholder was the novelist Enid Bagnold, who lived nearby at Rottingdean. Their weekly trips to Barnham Market by train, to sell produce and return with flapping ducks and sacks of feed, was the start of a long and satisfying friendship. Meanwhile Duff — still Chancellor of the Duchy of Lancaster — became head of the Security Executive, which covered, among other things, internment, the development of germ warfare, and plans to mislead the enemy. The most famous deception of all — the dropping of a body with fake plans for an invasion of Greece — he later used as the basis for his only novel, *Operation Heartbreak*.

Although still tainted with the Singapore *débâcle*, Duff remained remarkably philosophical. It was Diana who could not forgive the unfairness of it all. He was still liable to have one of his 'veiners' as his apoplectic furies were known, from time to time, but they were rarer and his friends remarked on this mellowing. In breaks from his work in London, he wrote another book, *David*, down at Bognor. This fictional biography of the Biblical king was admired by Wavell, to Duff's great satisfaction, and also sold well. But there was still no news of what he felt was a real job.

Churchill had in fact been trying hard to find Duff something in foreign affairs, but every suggestion was blocked by what Diana later called 'Anthony Eden's wheel-spoking ways'. Finally the Prime Minister suggested Duff's appointment as British Representative to the French Committee of National Liberation in Algiers. This time Eden did not object. He was having serious problems as a result of Churchill's exasperation with de

DUFF COOPER—*trying to make Americans believe in Germany's war guilt and forget England's war debts*

Gaulle and all things French. Duff, he realised, could be a very useful buffer, being probably the only person capable of deflecting Winston's phobia.

Encouraged by Brendan Bracken and Harold Macmillan, Duff decided to accept the post. He went down to Bognor to tell Diana. She was loath to abandon the little farm yet again, but never for a moment considered staying behind. She understood Duff's reasons for wanting this job, which promised the Paris Embassy as soon as France was liberated. He had tired of party politics and the idea of returning to diplomacy appealed to him.

On January 3, 1944, Duff and Diana were met at the Algiers airfield by de Gaulle's chief aide, Gaston Palewski. To begin with Diana hated the upheaval. She was miserably homesick for Bognor. And her mood was not helped by the improvised living conditions — 'ugliness of a colossal kind, combined with gloomy darkness, paralysing cold, and dusty, musty squalor'. In time, Diana so transformed the place that she looked back on it as a sun-bathed palace from the Thousand and One Nights, set in an enchanted garden.

Duff's role required even more self-control and tact than either of them had expected. Diana called him the 'oilman' reducing the friction between Churchill and de Gaulle, nicknamed Charlie Wormwood. And it certainly required all of her talents to rescue official dinners from excruciating silences when 'conversation flowed like glue'. Diana even got away with addressing de Gaulle in the familiar *tu* form. He had to put such unprecedented informality down to ignorance of the language.

At the beginning of June, just before D Day, Duff flew back to England with de Gaulle. Relations could hardly have been worse between Churchill and his *bête noire*, who was convinced, with some justification it must be said, that the English and Americans were scheming to prevent his leadership of France. The only consolation for Duff during this fraught period was Eden's unexpected friendliness and help.

On the very morning of the invasion Anglo-French relations reached their worst point, with de Gaulle's sudden refusal to send French liaison officers or to broadcast to his countrymen. Churchill's explosion of fury was terrifying. But fortunately, while Brendan Bracken restrained him, Duff managed to corner de Gaulle and persuade him to relent. It was undoubtedly the most crucial and effective intervention of his diplomatic career.

Once the Normandy beach heads were established, Duff returned to Algiers with de Gaulle. Diana was in Rome when she heard that Paris was liberated, and her uneasiness grew as she packed up in Algiers. 'There is a feeling of *fin de saison*,' she wrote, 'and that *saison* the last.'

In London, Diana stayed

> long enough to order some clothes suitable to Paris, not to me — what we called 'like other people' dresses and some humourless hats. No more clowning. I must try not to join the list of mad English ambassadresses.

Now that he had reached Paris, Duff was keen to cement an Anglo-French alliance. Diana, on the other hand, still preoccupied with Nanny's dictum that things didn't last for ever, could only see ends, never beginnings. For the last four years she had spent almost every day in trousers and funny hats. Now there was an obligation to look neat and soberly conventional at all hours. The freedom and happiness of Bognor and Algiers were behind her; and, more than anything else, Diana felt old.

Gradually, the clouds cleared. Diana was kept very busy with the Embassy, which had been neglected since the occupation. Once that was in order, her days were filled with embassy duties, the demands of formal entertaining, and her social life. Her clique of friends — '*La Bande* as we called this Comus-crew of artists' — would arrive at six in Diana's *Salon Vert*. At 7.30 she would disappear into her bedroom, bathe, change, and reappear to 'sweep the dear remnants down the backstairs', before her official guests arrived at the front door.

She started to enjoy the powers of her position, particularly the ability to provide what was scarce. When a lack of candles threatened to plunge the restaurant where she was dining into darkness, fresh ones were sent for from the Embassy. There was also whisky to dispense, and — in emergencies — penicillin. Diana's parties and eccentricities were famous — perhaps she was joining that list of mad English ambassadresses after all — but in the social life of post-war Paris she was a star, in a way she had not been since the early days of *The Miracle*. Her private guest list mixed oddly but successfully with official entertaining. Harold Nicolson, Noël Coward and Emerald Cunard helped liven parties of diplomats and grand officials, and few hostesses would have dared to bring Jean Cocteau and Winston Churchill together.

Duff, while still busy in his role of 'oilman', tried to devote himself to what he saw as the true purpose of his mission. Unlike Eden, who still seemed almost besotted with Stalin, he felt that peace could only be guaranteed by a European alliance built on an Anglo-French treaty. Britain, he argued, must play a leading part in a united continent; not retreat into isolation, depend overmuch on an unpredictable United States or remain tied to the notion of Empire. (Duff's clear view of the future during his Singapore days meant that he harboured no illusions of the sort so dear to Churchill.) Eden poured cold water on the European idea, at first suggesting it would only provoke the Russians. Duff did not miss the irony of such a reaction, from somebody who had come to see himself as the great anti-appeaser. But it was Churchill's reluctance to recognise de Gaulle's government and flat refusal to invite him to Yalta that caused the most immediate harm. Official dinners were interminable, with the General displaying 'his usual reluctance or inability to say anything pleasant'.

The result of the British elections of 1945 roused Diana's outrage at her country's ingratitude to Winston. Duff was less shocked. His own future under the new government looked distinctly uncertain, although Churchill's departure from office had at least removed one of the two millstones between which he had been crushed for so long. The other mill-

Right: 'The Rake's Progress' — a summer evening at Chantilly with John Julius and Duff.

stone, de Gaulle, left office abruptly in January 1946; but his successor Georges Bidault, who had been Foreign Minister, proved no less suspicious or obdurate. Duff's chance finally came during the short lived socialist administration of Léon Blum, the old Popular Front leader of 1936. A momentum towards a treaty was established, which even the return of Bidault did not deflect. On March 4, 1947 it was signed at the symbolically chosen town of Dunkirk.

Many people were surprised how well Duff got on with Ernest Bevin, the master of their fate. Susan Mary Patten, the wife of an American diplomat who became a great friend of both Duff and Diana's, described them together one weekend:

> Neither pretends to be what he isn't. Duff tells a story about Castlereagh and the Foreign Secretary says, 'That's a good one, who did you say he was?' and follows up with a coarse and funny story about something that happened in Glasgow in 1917 and Duff adores it and laughs heartily and Diana, sitting between them, knits away, looking incredibly beautiful. (*To Marietta from Paris*, Doubleday 1975)

She also observed of the old trades unionist:

> he is clearly in love with Diana, and implored her to come to Durham for the great miners' convention.

Duff's tasks during that last summer as ambassador included preparing for the Marshall Plan talks. Then, on September 3, the dreaded letter came. The Labour government could keep him on no longer. Duff was sad but resigned. As Bevin had written, he had had a good innings. Two and half years was far more than he had ever dared hope, considering he had been a political appointee. That night he and Diana left for Italy to console themselves for a few days. On December 10 they gave a memorable farewell party, for which Winston Churchill flew over from London, and a week later their friends assembled at the Gare du Nord to see them off.

Before the blow fell, Diana had found the ideal place for their retirement in the Château de Saint-Firmin, near Chantilly. As outgoing ambassador, Duff was not supposed to take up residence in France for at least a year, but they moved to Chantilly after only a token stay in England.

There, Diana's entertaining revived with scarcely a break. There were dinners of 24, of which one included Greta Garbo, Cecil Beaton and Princess Margaret, who sang and played the piano. The combination of guests at Chantilly gave rise to some unusual sights, such as Orson Welles and Lord Ismay (then Secretary General of NATO) picking lilies of the valley in the woods after lunch.

Duff had built a beautiful library in the Paris Embassy, and endowed it with the finest part of his collection of books. But he still had plenty left for Chantilly, where he settled down to a peaceful and productive existence. *Sergeant Shakespeare*, published in 1949, argued that Shakespeare had seen active service in the Low Countries with the Earl of Leicester. This was followed a year later by *Operation Heartbreak*. Duff was criticised for this novel, which many people saw as a betrayal of the spirit, if not the letter, of the Official Secrets Act. Duff defended himself by saying that what he had revealed was hardly a secret, since Winston had been holding dinner parties spell-bound with the story for years.

His last book was his autobiography, *Old Men Forget*, and he had the satisfaction of seeing it receive as much praise as his first, *Talleyrand*. There were plans for others, including a history of Venice, but he did not live to write them. In late 1953, after several illnesses, Duff became convinced that a winter in Jamaica at the invitation of Lord Brownlow would do him and Diana good. His doctor warned him of the voyage's dangers, with no nearby hospital if the illness struck again. But since he was feeling much better, Duff decided to ignore the advice. He died at sea, on New Year's Day.

Duff's nephew Rupert Hart-Davis had published his uncle's last three books; and it was he who persuaded Diana to start writing her memoirs, to take her mind off her grief. The third and final volume of her autobiography, *Trumpets from the Steep*, ends just before Duff's death with the implication that the rest of her life would be spent in quiet privacy.

> There will be no photographs of the slippered stage. Cecil Beaton, whose eyes are more dissecting than his flattering lens, must close his shutter. It opened last to portray me as Tiepolo's idea of Cleopatra at the famous Beistegui ball in Venice. The frontiers still let me through with that photograph in my passport. When they won't I'll stay at home.

Yet when Diana left Chantilly, she knew she faced two alternatives: either to live out her widowhood with familiar friends and old memories, or to build a new life for herself without Duff. The latter course seemed impossible at first — but the choice was not in doubt.

Right: Dressing up at Chantilly, with Artemis as the Lion.

Artemis   me

Above: Diana in Ethiopia, aged eighty.

1
DRESSING UP
1892–1910

*D*iana's mother Violet had very determined ideas about beauty, which were firmly rooted in a romanticised past. Everything bright, new and modern, including the bustles and buttoned boots of the day, was dismissed with a shudder as ugly and common. She also despised the fashion of heavy chignons, dressing her own hair *à la grecque* with the family tiara worn back to front for grand occasions. This prompted King Edward VII to remark that she never seemed to brush her hair. Her clothes — dyed in tea to relieve them of their glaring whiteness — fell in soft folds from a cinched waist, and she could never resist historical touches like tricorne hats, Florentine sleeves, or Byronic ruffles.

Violet's father, Colonel Charles Lindsay, had been a royal equerry, and in her youth she had often stayed at Balmoral. It was there that Queen Victoria painted her portrait in watercolour. As an artist, Violet was considerably better than one might have expected. Her cultivated tastes made her not only a founder member of the Souls, but also the friend of the leading writers, painters and dramatists of the day. Of these, the most important for Diana turned out to be her mother's friendship with Sir Herbert Beerbohm Tree and his family.

The Trees used to come to Belvoir Castle for Christmas, and Iris and Viola became Diana's life long friends. Duchess and children alike adored delving into the huge dressing up box to deck themselves out. Any excuse seemed good enough — charades, playlets, *tableaux vivants*, and sitting for portraits or photographs.

Diana's childhood had been a happy one, marred only by her illness and memories of her mother's grief at the death of her elder son Haddon. Being the baby of the family and 'delicate', Diana grew up indulged, but not spoilt. She was an affectionate child, holding Papa in the awed respect natural for the time. She admired her elder siblings enormously — John for his gravitas and photography, and Marjorie for her artistic talent. Letty was younger and more adventurous, and Diana followed her around with all the enthusiasm of a puppy.

Without any doubt the most important influence on Diana was her mother. 'I am not capable,' she wrote, 'of describing the extraordinary beauty and flavour that emanated from my mother. She had ethereal iridescence, passionate but not over-demonstrative love for her children, and a certain mysterious detachment.' Violet's daughters were brought up to move gracefully, and acquired a taste for the theatrical that was strongest in Diana. With her golden beauty, it was to be a devastating combination.

Previous page: Watercolour by Queen Victoria of Violet Lindsay at Balmoral, shortly before her marriage in 1882.

Above: Diana's brother John at Cockayne Hatley, their childhood home in the early 1890's.

Right: Harry Cust at Hatley, drawn by Diana's mother.

*Above: Diana's brother John
and sister Marjorie.*

*Right: Diana 'fretted by sallies
of her Mother's kisses'.*

Above: Henry Manners, 8th Duke of Rutland.

Left: The Duchess and John, in an uneasy mixture of medieval and Tudor costume.

Above: Diana in Carolean lace.

Right: Diana as Princess Katherine, and her sister Letty as the King, in 'Henry V'.

Opposite: Diana as Joan of Arc, drawn by Violet Rutland.

Diana as Joan of Arc.   15 years old

45

*Above: Watching autumn
manoeuvres in 1910: Violet
Rutland, Diana, Letty, Ruby
Lindsay, and Marjorie behind
on the running board.*

2
COMING OUT
AND THE COTERIE
1910–1914

When Diana came out in 1910, she can have had little time for fellow debutantes only able to talk of hunting and parties. Her wings and aspirations had grown precociously during those summers at Brancaster with the Beerbohm Trees; and the group of undergraduates she had met there was developing into a circle she christened the Corrupt Coterie. But however impatient Diana might have been with conventional contemporaries, she never shunned the company of her class.

It is interesting to see her at a race meeting with Nancy Cunard, who was to reject so vigorously the assumptions and politics of her upbringing. When Diana visited her later in the artistic ghetto known as Fitzrovia, she was fascinated and repelled by the promiscuity and Bohemian squalor. Such fastidiousness was almost a hallmark of the Coterie's members, who in spite of their pride in outrageous and dissipated behaviour were deeply traditional at heart. Their parents in the Souls had disdained the opulent decadence of the Marlborough House Set of King Edward VII. Instead of gambling, racing and adultery they pursued art, elevated conversation and rather ethereal love affairs. Their children, despite all their declamations, represented little more than a hot-blooded version of the Souls.

Life for a debutante with Diana's connections consisted of a round of balls, weddings, *tableaux vivants*, sittings for portraits and being entertained at the great country houses of Edwardian society. Such a programme required innumerable dresses. And with the parsimony instilled by her mother, Diana designed and made nearly all her own costumes as well as many for friends. This profitable little enterprise was based on the fashionable designs of Poiret and the Ballets Russes.

The Duchess often took Diana to gatherings of Souls and politicians at Hackwood, the home of Lord Curzon. Places like Maxine Elliott's house at Hartsbourne were much livelier. There, slightly tipsy, she was dazzled by Lord Rocksavage, one of the most beautiful young men of his day, whom Diana thought 'probably Apollo — anyhow some God'. That her mother would have warmly approved of such a match — Rocksavage was heir to the Marquess of Cholmondeley — was always likely to prove a dampener.

Diana moved on, men falling for her in droves. It was after all the age of Zuleika Dobson. Most of her willing victims were in the Coterie. Her triumphs are satirised by the photographic montage of Diana with a bow and Eddie Marsh as St Sebastian. Older men developed passions for her too, like Lord Wimborne, later the Lord Lieutenant of Ireland. The great Russian singer Feodor Chaliapin remained in love with her all his life. When he died his room was found to be full of photographs of Diana.

Although she had no intention of marrying for the moment, and was not tempted by the role of rural *châtelaine*, she was happy for her sisters. In February 1911, Diana was one of Letty's bridesmaids for her wedding to Ego Charteris, later Lord Elcho. Next came Marjorie's turn. Prince Felix Youssupov, subsequently the killer of Rasputin, had been desperately in love with her; but in August 1912, she married Charles, Marquess of Anglesey.

There was a wild intensity in the way the members of the Coterie lived

Previous page: Julian Grenfell, Diana's uncle Charles Lindsay, Letty, Marjorie with a cigarette, and John with a pipe.

48

their lives, as though they were subconsciously aware of the coming war that was to engulf them. Diana's great but hopeless love was for Raymond Asquith. Son of the Prime Minister and a brilliant lawyer, he had married Katherine Horner. Katherine was devoted to Diana, despite the latter's badly concealed feelings for Raymond. The poet Julian Grenfell has been described as part of the Coterie, though not as Diana saw it. She had little fondness for him, finding his arrogance unappealing. And to begin with she felt little, save a rather wary amusement, for Duff Cooper, whom she first met early in 1913.

That summer Diana was in Venice, where the Coterie — including Duff — shocked the inhabitants by dressing outlandishly, swimming across canals for bets, pretending to have fits in St Mark's Square, and throwing all night parties. They vowed to return the following year, but the war was to overtake them; and in a few years almost all of them were dead. 'Our generation,' wrote Duff in 1918, 'becomes history rather than growing up.'

Below: The Duke and Duchess at a meet of the Belvoir Hunt.

Opposite: Diana at the time she first met the Oxford forerunners of the Coterie at Brancaster.

Above: A fancy dress group photographed by the Baron de Meyer. Back: Lady Bingham, Herr Kuhlmann, Diana, Frau Kuhlmann. Front: Harry Paulton, Mrs Heneage, Baron Kuhn.

Left: Diana dressed in the style of Velasquez, another photograph by the Baron de Meyer.

*Opposite: Diana in a
photograph by her brother
John.*

*Right: Diana Stylites, ignored
by a Pekinese.*

*Left: As the Girl in 'Spectre de
la Rose'.*

Left: The Earl of Rocksavage in 1911, in the dress uniform of the 9th Lancers. He was considered the best looking man of his generation.

Will you take Lady Diana Manners in to dinner.

Right: Diana as a bridesmaid at Marjorie's marriage to Charles Anglesey, 1912.

Opposite top: Rivvy Grenfell (killed in September 1914), Diana and Letty at a point to point.

Opposite bottom: Diana and Nancy Cunard at the races.

Left: Diana's portrait of Feodor Chaliapin (or Charlie Pine, as she used to call him) drawn on the back of a menu and signed by him.

Below: One of Diana's dress designs, in the style of the Ballets Russes.

Left: Feodor Chaliapin as Boris Godounov.

56

Above: Diana's arrows piercing Eddie Marsh as
St Sebastian.

Diana   Juff   Katherine
                          asquith
        1913?

Coterie dressing up. Opposite: Diana, Duff and Katherine Asquith. Above: Duff and Clare Tennant. Right: Duff in Foreign Office attire.

Above: Julian Grenfell and Ego Charteris (Lord Elcho), just before the First World War.

3
LOVE AND WAR
1914–1919

1916

$\mathcal{E}$arly in October 1914, Diana signed on as a V.A.D. at Guy's Hospital. It was gruelling work, with eight hours of making beds, changing dressings and emptying bed-pans, and never a moment to sit down. She did not mind the Spartan conditions as much as the lack of free time to see her friends home on leave.

A few months later Diana was persuaded to leave Guy's and return to Arlington Street, which had been transformed into the Rutland Hospital for Officers. The work was not nearly as arduous as at Guy's; yet the Duchess was unhappy to find that although Diana was back at home, she seemed to see little more of her.

Diana was not the Duchess's only worry. Having borne the pain of losing one son, Violet Rutland was determined that the war should not rob her of the other. She enlisted the aid of George Moore, a rich American who besides being besotted with Diana was a close friend of Field Marshal Sir John French. Thanks to his intervention, John — despite his protests — became a staff officer. In January 1916 he married Kathleen Tennant, always known as Kakoo.

Encouraged by the Duchess's gratitude, George Moore continued to woo Diana with expensive presents. He was allowed little more than a hand to hold for his pains; but he was always prepared to throw the parties which Diana felt justified in requesting for the Coterie's brave warriors on leave.

Desperate to forget the trenches and only too aware of their mortality, these young men wanted to dance with pretty, cheerful women and drink themselves into oblivion. Diana was much criticised for her supposedly high spirits, at what became known as the 'dances of death'. But she had her supporters, too — one of whom was Winston Churchill. He wrote to his wife:

> The world has dealt harshly with her, but she is brave and hard-working and very misunderstood, and she is of great worth in this sad world. Why, the poor soldiers dying in agony whisper her name as they die.

When not nursing at Arlington Street, Diana was cooking supper for munitions workers with Katherine Asquith in the East End, taking part in *tableaux vivants* for war charities, or seeing her friends. Many weekends she spent with the Prime Minister and Margot Asquith at the Wharf or Walmer Castle. Other notable ones were at Chirk Castle in North Wales, which belonged to Margot Howard de Walden. Elaborate practical jokes were played, and dressing up in armour was thought a great 'stunt'. Hugo Rumbold managed to fool everyone by returning dressed as a woman, after his apparent departure for London; but then he was already famous for having accompanied his love of the moment on a long tour of Europe disguised as her maid.

Diana's 'Saturday to Mondays' were more respectable than some of her weekday haunts, which included Soho restaurants and the notorious Cavendish Hotel. These outings were kept from the Duchess, who was a nervous and protective mother, but one cannot help suspecting she turned a blind eye at times.

Above: As Britannia in one of her many patriotic tableaux vivants.

Previous page: Nurse Manners, in the uniform designed by the Duchess for the Rutland Hospital for Officers.

The hardest blow of the war came in 1916, when Raymond Asquith was killed. He had meant more to Diana than anyone, and after his death she became increasingly dependent on Duff. Their affection for each other deepened into love, as the war dragged on. By the time he was released from the Foreign Office in the summer of 1917, to begin training as an officer cadet in the Guards, all Diana had left of her dearest friends was their letters, and the photographs they had given her before leaving for the front.

She saw Duff off to France in April 1918, and then returned to Guy's where the long hours and exhausting work would numb the pain of their separation. They wrote every day, and Diana thought of nothing but his safety. Yet their courtship remained so discreet that only Alan and Viola Parsons, who had been let into the secret, knew of its existence.

Below: As Vermeer's Lady Reading a Letter.

When Diana finally screwed up enough courage to tell her mother that she wanted to marry Duff, the resulting hysteria made her feel 'like a murderess'. The next few months were tense and strained for them both, as the Duchess clutched at straws to avert the inevitable. Her daughter was constantly being sat next to eligible young men, and at a ball the Rutlands gave for Queen Marie of Roumania in March 1919, Diana was put beside the Prince of Wales. The miracle the Duchess had hoped for did not materialise: Diana told the Prince about Duff and their plans, and he wished them luck and happiness.

A month later her mother gave in, and the wedding was set for June 2. Her trousseau, though generous, was depressingly sensible — designed for life on a budget. Yet such was the quantity and magnificence of the wedding presents that they could scarcely be contained in the Arlington Street drawing room.

The day itself was unclouded; Diana remembered the nervous wait in the library, immobilised under her huge tulle veil. Then came the drive to St Margaret's Westminster with the Duke. Their car had to slow to a snail's pace to make its way through the crowds around the church. The bells were pealing triumphantly as she came out into the sunshine on Duff's arm, and the children of Viola and Alan Parsons scattered rose petals at their feet. The crowds, surging forward to get a better look, had to be held back by mounted police. Duff could not resist commenting that 'Diana's popularity with the mob is only comparable with that of Kitchener'.

Opposite: 'Myself as Russia for Charity'.

Chirk Castle 1916: Left, Viola Parsons in armour, embracing Diana.

Below: Viola Parsons being slain by Hugo Rumbold, while Diana and Margot Howard de Walden look on. Bottom: Diana, the painter Philip Wilson Steer, and Margot Howard de Walden.

Edward Horner (above) whom many thought secretly engaged to Diana. Ego, Lord Elcho (above right) the husband of Diana's sister Letty. Raymond Asquith (right), the son of the Prime Minister, and the man Diana most admired in the world. All three were killed in the First War.

Opposite: The actress Lily Elsie and Diana in 'Hearts of the World', a propaganda film by D. W. Griffith.

Left: Diana and Alan Parsons, who alone with his wife Viola, shared Diana's secret.

Right: Duff in uniform, 1918.

*The Duke and Diana, and (below) John and his wife
Kathleen Tennant, always known as Kakoo, in the
dining room at Arlington Street.*

Above: Queen Marie of Rumania in her coronation robes.

Friday, May 2, 1919,

LADY DIANA MANNERS BETROTHED.

ONE OF ENGLAND'S INTERESTING GIRLS TO WED AN OFFICER.

Lady Diana Manners, third and youngest daughter of the Duke and Duchess of Rutland, is to be wedded on June 2 to Lieut. Alfred Duff Cooper, D.S.O., cousin of Princess Arthur of Connaught, his mother being Lady Agnes Cooper, sister of the late Duke of Fife.

The honeymoon (says the "Daily Sketch") will be spent at Lord Grimthorpe's house at Naples.

Meredith's Diana was her spiritual godmother. Perhaps the then Lady Granby, watching the lovely droop of her baby's pink mouth and the set of her great grey eyes, divined somehow that

she, too, would one day be "a woman to kin[dle] poets and heroes, the princes of the race"; woman for a place in song, exalted to the ski[es]. Anyhow, with her immortal namesake, [she]

is never described as being either tall or short— proof that she is just the size most of us think a woman ought to be.

"Dressing-Up" Talent.

It was back in the pleasure hunting year of King George's Coronation that Lady Diana's talent for dressing up, for getting into a period, first became known to the wider public. Some of us best remember, from out of all the jewelled and colourful jumble of the Elizabethan tourney of that ye[ar] ... [de]mure figure in dark velvet, who looked was not a ... ... dern, but ... the great as she g[ave] ... dance, a[nd] ... gone bac[k] ...

Since ... ance ha[s] ... Manner[s] ... have c ... posed ... has be[en] ... saint, ... a co[stume] ... Nigh[tingale] ... whos[e] ... et ... tha[t] ... abl[e] ...

he ... de ... cl ...

LADY DIANA MANNERS.

my wedding 1919

Daily Mail
June 3

THE GOLDEN BRIDE.

LADY DIANA'S CARRIAGE STORMED BY WOMEN.

ROSE PETALS FROM CHILDREN.

On the face of things one would imagine that for the marriage of a beautiful and popular girl most of the sightseers would be men. Perhaps one in fifty of those assembled yesterday outside St. Margaret's, Westminster, to see Lady Diana Manners drive up and Lady Diana Duff Cooper drive away were men. It was essentially a woman's affair, a sub-conscious tribute, perhaps, by women to one of their sex who has become as legendary as many a goddess of mythology.

Ever since she was a golden-curled school girl Lady Diana has shone as the fairest and most brilliant English girl of the age. She became a sort of symbolic figure for countless women and girl admirers and she was the joy and delight of every social function. When the war came many a charity owed much to Lady Diana and many a wounded man, no less, to her cotside ministrations. And then this daughter of the Duke of Rutland gave her hand to an officer in the Guards—Lieut. Duff Cooper, a D.S.O. winner. And this was her wedding day.

The crowd was in places ten and twelve deep. It had begun to gather early in the morning. It was a strangely excited crowd of women, old and young, in every station of life, girls in the Services and women in rich attire. "I've put on my Sunday best for Lady Di," said one rather forlorn-looking little woman. . . . there seemed to be a deal behind that compliment. As Big Ben chimed the quarters and the preliminary wedding peal rang out at two o'clock, the serried ranks of women strained forward on tiptoe—when a whole crowd gets on tiptoe the result is nil, but no matter—and passed the guests in critical review.

Half-past two. The bells peal forth.

Right: Diana's attendants:
Martin (later Lord) Charteris,
Lady Caroline Paget, and
Martin's brother David, Lord
Elcho (later Earl of Wemyss and
March).

Martin   Caroline   David

Going Away after the reception
at Arlington Street. The
wedding night was spent at
Port Lympne, the house of
Philip Sassoon (below).

Above: Diana with her pages, Letty's sons David and Martin, at Arlington Street.

4
FILM STAR
1920–1923

The NOVEMBER
Picturegoer
Monthly 1/net
VOL.2. Nº11 1921

Lady Diana Manners

PHOTO BY LALLIE CHARLES

$\mathscr{T}$he Plan' to get Duff out of the Foreign Office and into politics required considerably more money than they possessed. Their style of life, to which Duff's superiors took exception, certainly appeared an arithmetical impossibility on their income. Diana explained this miracle in her memoirs:

> We lived above our means and were never in debt. This marvellous achievement was due to a reconciled and loving family, good friends, treats, foreign holidays, Paris jaunts, dresses without bills (first Ospovat, later Molyneux, faithful till our retirement, Chanel and Patou). Blind to my fantastic luck in these worldly ways, I did not consider it wonderful. Clothes were only trappings, and useful for our treats, but I could have managed perfectly with my needle and a fashion paper.

The 'treats' included Cap Ferrat, where an outing to Monte Carlo netted nearly £200 at *chemin de fer*; and then two holidays in Deauville at the invitation of Lord Wimborne, where they were joined by Diana's other admirer, Max Beaverbrook.

The answer to their financial problems came unexpectedly, almost three years after their first great opportunity collapsed through bad luck. During the war Diana had appeared in a propaganda film called *The Hearts of the World* directed by D. W. Griffith. Griffith described her as 'the most beloved woman in England', and in 1919 he offered her the leading role in a new film at a fee of $75,000. The upheaval of her wedding and honeymoon, followed by the accident which broke her leg, thwarted the project, and Griffith had to find another star. *Variety* magazine, however, suggested that Queen Mary herself had forbidden the stage to a duke's daughter.

In 1922, a director called John Stuart Blackton managed to raise the money for two films in England, having previously failed in the United States. He signed up Diana for both of them and ensured that her name and face were exploited to the full. Recognising the need for this publicity, Diana accepted the press's obsession with her beauty and rank as inevitable — and funny, when her hat or her profile was inflated into a matter of public debate.

Her first film, *The Glorious Adventure*, was a Restoration melodrama, set against a background of the plague and the Great Fire of London. Her co-star was the famous Australian prize-fighter, Victor McLaglen, and the contrast between the two provided a rich source for publicity. In the second film, *The Virgin Queen*, Diana played Elizabeth I. It is an indication of her box-office power that, when she was working on this film, more than half a dozen articles appeared on the question of whether or not her eyebrows had been removed for the part.

Such professionalism on the part of a duke's daughter caused what might seem an undue amount of interest; though even in the early nineteen-twenties, an officer in a fashionable regiment would have had to resign his commission on marrying an actress. In Diana's case, reactions were mixed. Some admired her for her pioneering spirit, but stuffier members of the middle class who liked their aristocracy on pedestals were scandalised. 'You THING, you!' wrote one poisonous pen. Her more obsessive critics invested her with all the qualities of the Scarlet Woman, but her next and most important role was to take her to the opposite extreme.

In 1923, not daring to believe her good fortune, Diana was summoned to Salzburg to audition for the part of the Madonna in Max Reinhardt's new production of *The Miracle*. There, she and Duff were lodged in his baroque palace of Leopoldskron. And to make her feel more at home, Reinhardt invited her friend Lord Berners, accompanied by the Sitwells and William Walton. For a couple of days, the impresario watched and waited, while Diana grew increasingly nervous. When he finally auditioned her, Reinhardt was impressed. Not only did she have a natural grace, but her eyes filled with tears as he told the story of the play. That night, the part was hers.

Duff and Diana set off for Venice to celebrate. It was their first visit since the Coterie's final summer there exactly ten years before. The familiar sights must have produced strange feelings — a mixture of nostalgia and loss as well as gratitude for their extraordinary luck.

Opposite: Lady Beatrice Fair (Diana) warned by Samuel Pepys (Lennox Pawle) not to disappoint Charles II in 'The Glorious Adventure', and (below) defending her virtue from the Monarch (William Luff).

Left: Diana maltreated by her co-star, the champion pugilist Victor McLaglen.

LADY DIANA MANNERS.

March 11, 1922.

THE FILM RENTER & MOVING PICTURE NEWS.

33

HOW I MALTREATED LADY DIANA.

By Victor McLaglen.

The noted former boxer, who once fought Jack Johnson and had many thrilling ring encounters, holding the championship of the Pacific North-west, and now a successful screen actor, tells of his experiences in film work with the beautiful Lady Diana Manners.

EVERYONE is asking me how a big, strong fellow like myself could have handled the delicately beautiful Lady Diana Manners so roughly as I did in Mr. J. Stuart Blackton's photoplay, "The Glorious Adventure." Well, it was not easy, I'll say that. There, before me, was the most lovely type of feminine beauty I have ever seen, with that fragile quality which appeals to a man's protective instinct. I'd have preferred to play the hero part, but the scenario said

remembering the beautiful bride of the midnight ceremony, went to claim her as my own. After that I had to treat the sweet lady most shamefully.

The Director Urged Me On.

I tried to soften my feeling, but there was always the director urging me on to renewed villainy. " Camera! " he would call, and as the deadly clicking sounded I would walk on and face the beautiful Lady Diana, who made it all the more difficult for me because of her realistic expressions of fear and horror of me. " Go on, Victor! " Mr. Blackton would call out, " Remember you're a brutish felon without mercy! " And so I had to maul around the delicate young woman. Mr. Blackton would so arouse me that my old instinct of the fighting ring would be brought out, and I would go through a scene and almost collapse at the end through fear of having severely bruised Lady Diana.

But she would nurse a sore wrist or a twisted shoulder and smilingly assure me it was all right.

Previous Pugilistic Encounters.

I can assure you that acting these scenes with Lady Diana was more worrying to me than any fight I ever had in the ring with any of the world-renowned pugilists. When I faced Jack Johnson at Vancouver, B.C., in 1909, I had no fear. I was his first opponent after he won the world championship. It was a six-round, no-decision contest. The year before that I had fought Erail Schock at Aberdeen, Wash., for the championship of the Pacific North-west, and won in twenty rounds. The same year I fought a draw with Ed. Martin at Aberdeen, Wash. Martin had also fought a draw with Johnson. I knocked out Ted Boyden in the second round in a fight at San Francisco in 1911, and the following year beat Sailor White in three rounds in New York.

But, again, I say that none of these fighting adventures caused me half the worry that I felt when I had to fight Lady Diana in " The Glorious Adventure."

SCENE FROM " THE GLORIOUS ADVENTURE."

that I must treat her rough, and the director was right on the job with instructions that I was to get all excited and vicious, and knock the heroine around.

Ill-Treating the Heroine.

Mr. Blackton is not a producer whose instructions an actor can disobey or change to suit his own taste. He told me I had to abuse Lady Diana most awfully, and there was nothing else to do. There it was in the scenario—scene after scene of horrible treatment of the sweet heroine.

And Lady Diana stood there, looking beautiful in seventeenth century gowns, and the last person in the world a man could wish to abuse. But she was really sporting, and entered fully into the spirit of the scenes. Many times I paused to apologise or to express a wish that my rough realism would not be unpleasant to her, but she would reply with a soft laugh and beg me not to worry on her account.

You see, I was a criminal

THE GLORIOUS ADVENTURE (Blackton, Stoll, Deal, Griffin).—Society has described Lady Diana Manners as a woman of startling beauty. It is hard to say why, because the fair Lady Diana has a very long face, and a rather ungainly bony body. Her acting is very amateurish and awkward, and in our personal opinion there are only two or three instances where she is passable. For example, when she has the interview with King Charles at Whitehall, she is at her best, but this is due rather to the acting of King Charles and the skill of the Director. For Stewart Blackton, we have nothing but the highest praise. He has put before the world a remarkable film, which marks an entirely new phase in the development of the cinematograph industry. Some of the colouring is not quite what it should be, but on the whole the picture is a very fine historical masterpiece, in natural tints, and Victor McLaglen as the condemned felon contributes a most impressive performance. Every part entrusted to recognised screen artists, as distinct from a Society favourite, is exceedingly well cast and well played, and the scenes depicting the Fire of London are magnificently carried out. Though Lady Diana Manners is, in our opinion, a drawback to the picture rather than an asset, and though the Prizmatic photographic methods have not yet attained perfection, we have no hesitation in designating "The Glorious Adventure" one of the greatest money-makers which showmen have been able to secure for some time. We therefore advise our readers to book it and boom it ambitiously.

The Most Beautiful Profile?

Is this the world's most beautiful profile? John Elvin, an English artist, who has travelled the world over, declares that his portrait of Lady Diana Manners, daughter of the Duke and Duchess of Rutland, reproduced herewith, shows her to be the finest profile he has ever seen. Lady Diana plays the leading role in the J. Stuart Blackton natural colour film, "The Glorious Adventure," released this week throughout the United Kingdom.

UNE DUCHESSE AU CINÉMA

LADY DIANA MANNERS est la plus jeune des trois délicieuses filles du duc et de la duchesse de Rutland, qui, elle-même, a été une des plus jolies femmes d'Angleterre. Les sœurs de lady Diana sont la marquise d'Anglesey et lady Violet Benson.

Depuis Mme Récamier, aucune femme de la société n'avait joint à la beauté une personnalité aussi intéressante et n'avait soulevé une admiration aussi générale que lady Diana. Non seulement elle a une taille de jeune déesse et un visage exquis, mais son intelligence remarquable et son sens artistique en font une créature d'exception et nul ne peut la voir sans rester sous le charme de cette jeune femme, mince, élancée, aux cheveux d'or et aux yeux bleus. Elle évoque tellement les plus purs antiques qu'un grand nombre de peintres et de sculpteurs sont venus de tous les coins du monde pour avoir l'honneur de la prendre comme modèle.

par sa beauté, mais par son esprit et il n'est pas douteux que le terme " incarner un rôle " n'aura jamais été plus pleinement exact que dans le nouvel essai de lady Diana... Elle aura d'ailleurs

LADY DIANA MANNERS RAPPELLE PAR SA GRACE ET SA BEAUTÉ Mme RÉCAMIER

bien peu d'efforts à faire pour créer autour d'elle l'ambiance nécessaire ; n'a-t-elle pas passé toute une partie de sa vie entre les murailles historiques de ce Haddon Hall où vécut Dorothy Vernon il y a quatre siècles.

Ayant prouvé dans sa première apparition à l'écran qu'elle possédait un incontestable talent, lady Diana tient cependant à se pénétrer plus

un coup de baguette magique, nous fera revivre à l'époque fastueuse d'Élisabeth d'Angleterre.

Ce n'est pas la première fois qu'une personnalité mondaine aborde la carrière d'artiste cinématographique. Depuis quelques années, on compte, dans les studios de Berlin, de Los Angeles un certain nombre de princes russes, de grandes dames de la noblese pétersbourgeoise ou mosco-

WORLD'S BEAUTY STARS IN FILM COMING TO S. F.

Lady Diana Manners Has Leading Part in Glorious Adventure

FEATURE AT GRANADA

First Picture to Be Entirely Made by Prizma Process

By GEORGE C. WARREN

San Francisco motion picture enthusiasts and others will have an opportunity next week, beginning Saturday, to compare Lady Diana Manners, said to be the most beautiful living Anglo-Saxon woman in the world, with beauties that are around us here in California.

The type is similar. California women live the outdoor life that the English women live; have the same sort of complexions; are for the most part rangy creatures, like their English sisters, and they understand the art of dress to a far greater degree than the women of Britain.

Lady Diana, long noted as an amateur actress, after a long battle with her parents, the Duke and Duchess of Rutland, and with Queen Mary of England, obtained consent

English Beauty

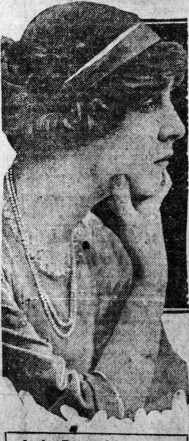

Lady Diana Manners, acclaimed by artists as the most beautiful Anglo-Saxon woman in the world.

LADY DIANA MANNERS UNDERSTUDYING MARY PICKFORD.

THE·RULES·OF·THE GAME
by LADY·DIANA·COOPER

Left: Illustrated heading to one of Diana's many articles — usually written by Duff.

Exclusive Exhibition Rights Controlled By
The Rose Film Company Ltd.
89-91 Wardour St. London, W.1.

THE VIRGIN QUEEN

J. Stuart Blackton's
super production
in natural colour.
featuring
LADY DIANA MANNERS

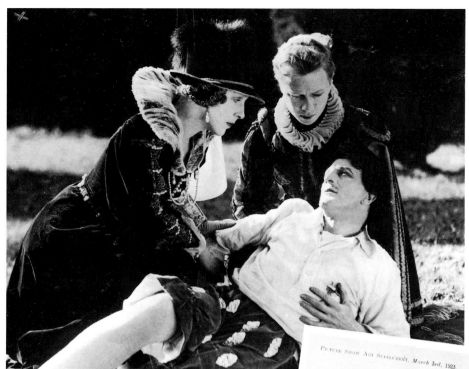

Above: Queen Elizabeth (Diana) and Lord Darnley (Sir Francis Laking) come to the aid of Borghese (A. B. Imeson) in 'The Virgin Queen'.

PICTURE SHOW ART SUPPLEMENT, March 3rd, 1923.

MARY ARUNDEL
(Marian Blackton).

PRESTALL THE ASTROLOGER
(Tom Haselwood).

BISHOP DE QUADRA
(William Luff).

MARY QUEEN OF SCOTS
(Maisie Fisher).

LETTICE KNOLLYS
(Violet Virginia Blackton).

LORD ROBERT DUDLEY (Carlyle Blackwell).

QUEEN ELIZABETH
(Lady Diana Manners).

(Stuart Blackton.)

COUNTESS OF LENNOX
Norna Whalley).

SIR WILLIAM CECIL (Hubert Carter).

Left: Diana, Max Beaverbrook, and Duff 'snapshotted on the beach at Deauville, where all society is congregated at the moment'.

Right: Duff, Diana, and Lord Wimborne, touring in France.

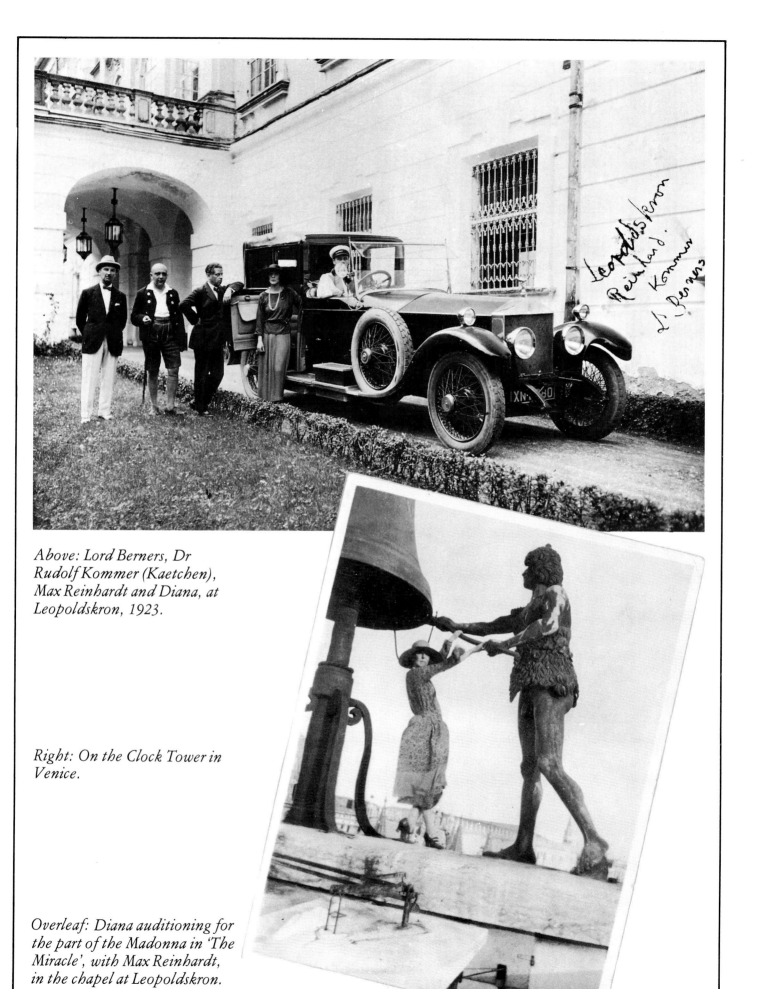

Above: Lord Berners, Dr
Rudolf Kommer (Kaetchen),
Max Reinhardt and Diana, at
Leopoldskron, 1923.

Right: On the Clock Tower in
Venice.

Overleaf: Diana auditioning for
the part of the Madonna in 'The
Miracle', with Max Reinhardt,
in the chapel at Leopoldskron.

5
THE MIRACLE
1923–1928

*D*iana and Duff sailed to the United States on the *Aquitania* in November 1923. Halfway across, telegrams of welcome began to arrive from friends in New York, but also some disturbing instructions from *The Miracle*'s publicity director, Morris Gest. If asked how she knew she was going to play the Madonna on the first night, Diana was to say that God had told her she was to act His Mother.

Diana had no intention of saying anything so absurd, but she could not escape the embarrassing fact that two people had been engaged to act the Madonna: herself, and Maria Carmi, Princess Matchiabelli, who had created the role in C. B. Cochran's original production. Carmi did not know that she was the fallback, in the event of Diana not coming up to expectations. Gest whipped up the rivalry between them into a 'battle of the stars' to keep up the interest of the press, for the conversion of the Century Theatre into a medieval cathedral was taking far longer than expected.

Duff returned to England after two weeks, still unsure who would play the Madonna on the opening night. The decision was made in a draw for the benefit of the press in early January. Diana found it deeply distasteful, since by then she knew that the draw had been rigged in her favour. *The Miracle* opened on January 14, and her performance made her a star overnight.

During the desperate rush of dress-rehearsals, Reinhardt still found time to rehearse Diana in the role of the Nun, which was complementary to that of the Madonna. The part demanded restless energy rather than static grace, but the critics were equally enthusiastic. She continued to play the Nun from time to time; but the role was usually taken by Rosamund Pinchot, the eighteen year old daughter of an American senator, and later by Iris Tree.

The success of the show was so great that Diana was faced with the prospect of staying with *The Miracle* for longer than the sixteen weeks she had signed up for. Financial considerations won, but her exhausting schedule and the months without Duff made it a hard decision. She spent the winter season of the next four years touring America with *The Miracle*.

Although Diana was often lonely, there were friends. Rudolf Kommer, Reinhardt's right hand man had been devoted to her ever since her arrival at Leopoldskron. His round face and velvety voice provided a reassuring presence for Diana across the continent. She was delighted when, in 1925, her old friend Iris Tree joined the production as the Nun. Iris was usually in love and in trouble, and always broke, but she made life on tour infinitely more fun.

Kommer, or Kaetchen as they called him, developed an obsessive devotion to the two leading ladies; and he bitterly regretted the day he allowed Raimund von Hofmannsthal to join the company. The son of the poet and librettist Hugo von Hofmannsthal, who was a close friend of Reinhardt's, Raimund was working his passage across America as an extra earning $30 a week. It was bad enough that Iris and Diana should treat him to supper in their rooms, for Kaetchen did not approve of favouritism in such a large cast. But when he found out that the three of them had gone off secretly on holiday in Arizona, he was sick with jealousy.

The Duchess of Rutland joined *The Miracle* on tour in 1924, and enjoyed herself so much that she returned for an even longer stay the following year. Diana found her company a mixed blessing. Her drawings of back-stage life made her popular with the cast, but her public pronouncements could be embarrassing, such as the time she told a newspaper that her daughter had only gone on stage because she was so poor. As Diana complained to Duff,

> It's a thing she has been begged not to do, and warned that it's very bad for our good names — as Americans despise poverty. We don't after all get free rooms and motors out of pity, but because we are thought grand and important.

Diana enjoyed America; but her enthusiasm for drug-stores, cowboys, and New York skyscrapers, was never shared by Duff. The only way to see him meant a return to Europe by liner.

OLE CLAIMED BY TWO STARS; WAR FORECAST

Italian Princess Arrives in U. S. to Play "Madonna" in The Miracle.

SAYS SHE WAS HIRED

Lady Diana Manners Already Rehearsing Part for Revival.

NEW YORK, Dec. 11.—A c[...] tween two titled stars of t[...] which will surpass in magn[...] famous Mary Garden - Lina[...] controversy of 20 years ag[...] dicted on Broadway tonig[...] arrival of Princess Nor[...] belli of Italy to claim the rol[...] donna" in The Miracle, for which Mrs[...] Duff Cooper, the former Lady Diana Manners, already is rehearsing.

"Of course I shall play the Madonna[...]

LADY DIANA SHOOS WOLF.

Poverty Drove Her to Stage, Says Mother, En Route Here.

Special Cable to The World

SOUTHAMPTON, Dec. 12.—Pity the poor working girl! Poverty has driven Lady Duff-Cooper, better known as Lady Diana Manners, to take up her career on the stage and screen. Her mother, the Duchess of Rutland, admitted this to-day just before sailing on the Berengaria to join her daughter, who is in New York.

Asked if Lady Diana would make other theatrical engagements in America other than to play in "The Miracle," the Duchess replied:

"It depends on the offers received. She is very poor, and but for that you would never have seen her on the screen."

Copyright (New [...]

PROMINENT PEOPLE.

No. 19.—LADY DIANA DUFF COOPER.

Famous as a Society beauty, and daughter of the Earl of Rutland, Lady Diana Duff Cooper has again achieved fame on the occasion of her latest appearance in C. B. Cochran's amazing stage spectacle, "The Miracle." "Lady Di" appeared in the previous production in New York in 1924, and she then created a sensation with her Madonna-like beauty, which in itself made her ideal for the part. One of her ordeals is to pose as a statue of the Madonna without moving for half an hour. She has played the part in ten towns in U.S.A., and five on the Continent.

Lady Diana Cooper was Lady Diana Manners before her marriage in 1919 to Captain Alfred Duff Cooper, D.S.O., who is Financial Secretary to the War Office, and their house is the scene of many notable social and political gatherings.

Film-goers will doubtless remember "Lady Di's" earlier excursions into the film world, when, under the direction of J. Stuart Blackton, a pioneer of the industry, she made two pictures—one of them among the earliest films in colour—in which she played the role of Queen Elizabeth.

Opposite: The Duchess sketching her daughter backstage.

Above: Werner Krauss as the Spielmann, seducing Diana as the Nun.

No. 3. Lady Diana Duff-Cooper refusing to be interviewed.

Cleveland U.S.A. 1924

The profile of Lady Diana Duff Cooper (Lady Diana Manners) has been set to music by Professor Dayton S. Miller, of the Case School of Applied Science, Cleveland, Ohio, in the form of a chord.

Lady Diana's "face chord" is not a fanciful invention, but a scientific transcript of wireless waves corresponding to the curves of the profile.

Professor Miller invented an instrument for photographing sound waves, which are carried to a diaphragm that oscillates a mirror. He found that some of the curves produced by musical sounds bore a resemblance to the human profile, and argued that if a combination of musical sounds produced a photographic resemblance to a human profile, then, the process being reversed, the human profile should produce musical sounds.

A photograph of an actress was placed in a projector and thrown on a sheet of paper. The profile was traced and reduced, by means of a "harmonic analyser," into its simplest component musical curves. They numbered fourteen.

Fourteen organ pipes that were known to give similar curves were sounded before the photographing apparatus, and on the sensitised film there appeared the profile of the young woman, which is said to be as perfect as the original. The musical notes representing the profile were thus discovered.

A Wireless Sketch of Lady Diana.

Top: Diana at one of the luncheons in her honour, while on tour with 'The Miracle'.

Above: On tour, accompanied by Morris Gest and her uncle, Harry Lindsay.

93

'Miracle' Stars Arrive, Three With Bobbed Hair

Lady Diana Manners, the Madonna, Finds Short Tresses Quite Comfortable—Likes Americans and Cafeterias.

When the stars of "The Miracle" arrived in St. Louis yesterday, one thing was proved, that bobbed hair is not out of fashion. Lady Diana Manners, famed English beauty; Miss Iris Tree, daughter of the late actor-manager Sir Herbert Beerbohm Tree, and Miss Elinor Patterson of Chicago, each as she alighted from the New York train exhibited a bob.

"It is much more comfortable this way," said Lady Diana, "and I have no thought of letting it grow, at least for a long time."

Lady Diana, who created the roles of the Madonna and the Nun in "The Miracle," which opens at the Coliseum Christmas Eve, and two alternates in the role of the Nun, were welcomed by the St. Louis Miracle Committee and whisked to a suite at Hotel Chase, which will be their home through Christmas and the four weeks of "The Miracle" engagement here. With them was the dowager Duchess of Rutland, mother of Lady Diana and her constant companion during the past two months.

Daughter of Duke of Rutland.

Lady Diana is the youngest ... of the eighth Duke of ...

be on display at the Newho... Galleries, 484 North Kings... way boulevard, beginning t... row.

Schuyler Ladd, who pl... Prince, and Fritz Feld, th... leading male roles in "The... arrived on an earlier train... and were on hand to w... other stars. Both men c... roles when the Americ... tion opened in New... has a long career... Max Reinhardt's par... ing played the pip... productions with N... Nun. A third alte... beth Schirmer, an... producer, are ex...

The stars expre... the idea of playing a gu... ance to the children of St. ... guests of the Post-Dispatch Christ... mas Festival Association, on Christ... mas afternoon.

Splendid, Says Lady Diana.

Lady Diana asked particularly if the children would be of an age to appreciate the pantomime, and assured that they were, wanted the additional assurance that the younger children would be fittingly...

LADY DIANA MANNERS AND MISS TREE LIKED WALL PAPERS OF HOTEL

Former Plans to Add American Room to London Home; Came to Salem Chiefly to Inspect Antiques; Many Visits Made

Lady Diana Manners and her friend, Miss Iris Tree, both principals in "The Miracle," the famous dramatic production now being staged in this city, were visitors in Boston, They spent several hours about Sa-lem. Their coming was unheralded, so the noted English stage stars had a rather quiet time of it, which seemed to please them. They were accompanied by L. C. Prior, manager of the Hotel Lenox at Boston, and a Mr. Comar, a representative of the theatrical interests staging th fa-...

lishment in the hotel, took the eye of the visitors and they also visited that place. They tried on many hats. It is reported that Lady Diana was much attracted by one of the hats.

A bottle of face lotion was pur-chased and then the ladies made their way out to the hotel lobby and the dining hall.

Leaving the dining hall, the visitors walked out of the hotel and up to the Essex Institute. There they met Miss Sally Etheridge and examined mate-rial there. Later they took Miss Etheridge with them and motored to...

The Madonna.
Diana Manners.

First
telephone call
Hollywood
London

1927

*Opposite top: Gertrude von
Hofmannsthal, Iris Tree, Hugo
von Hofmannsthal and his son
Franz, and Diana, in Salzburg
1925. Diana had just persuaded
Max Reinhardt to take on Iris as
the Nun. The following year,
Diana and Iris (above), with
Raimund von Hofmannsthal
who had just joined the cast,
went on holiday in Arizona and
(right) Diana making her first
transatlantic telephone call,
aided by Morris Gest.*

Above: On a studio set in Hollywood. Back: Kaetchen Kommer, Max Reinhardt, unidentified, Capt. Alistair MacIntosh, Constance Talmadge. Centre: Joseph Schenck, Count Carpegna, the Duchess of Sermonetta, Mary Pickford, unidentified, Diana. Front: John Barrymore, unidentified, Douglas Fairbanks Sr.

6
ESCAPE FROM
THE STATES
1924–1928

*A*fter two disappointments, Duff was chosen in 1924 as Conservative candidate for Oldham in Lancashire. Diana, who had forced Morris Gest to agree to her absence from *The Miracle* in the event of a general election, returned to England to be at Duff's side for the campaign.

Remembering the stormy days of their engagement, Diana was very pleased by the way her family gave Duff their full support during the election. Yet however great their efforts, it was Diana's presence that attracted the publicity needed, and her warmth amply made up for Duff's shy diffidence off the platform. The mill-girls gave her a particularly enthusiastic reception:

> The girls mobbed me and kissed me, and thought me funny. I promised them a clog-dance if they put my husband in.

The intensity of the campaign and Diana's role was shown by the strenuous protests of Duff's opponents when a local cinema featured *The Virgin Queen*.

Duff won handsomely, and Diana performed her clog dance. They were received at Belvoir in triumph, where the Duke had them installed in the King's Rooms — the best in the house. 'The Plan', Diana wrote, 'was no longer a blueprint. The elevation was rising.'

Their lives now settled into a pattern. Diana's American tours separated them during the winter months and for the summer they were reunited: in London when the House was sitting, then in France or Italy during the recess. Although Diana was an adventurous traveller, Duff preferred to visit places where there was plenty of good food, wine and hot water. Paris and Venice were favourite haunts, as was San Vigilio: a small hotel by the water's edge on Lake Garda, which they discovered by accident and returned to again and again.

In January 1928, Eric and Rosemary Ednam (later the Earl and Countess of Dudley) invited them on a long trip to Biskra in the Sahara, which Duff joined with considerable misgivings. There, they 'rode in the desert and ate on eiderdowns under palms with Clare Sheridan and sheiks and bushagas'. Diana adored it; but when Duff received a telegram offering him the post of Financial Secretary to the War Office, he was probably grateful for the chance to leave in a hurry.

Reinhardt closed his production of *The Miracle* with a European tour in 1928. He wanted to work with Diana again, and she also had offers from John Barrymore and Diaghilev. But she turned them all down to resume her life with Duff.

That winter, Diana went to the Bahamas on the invitation of Michael Herbert, who with his brother Sidney often spent the winter in Nassau. She and Duff had accompanied them on a previous trip, but this time Diana went alone. The holiday was ruined by a nervous, uneasy sickness that she correctly diagnosed as pregnancy, and in September 1929, Duff and Diana's only son John Julius was born.

Previous page: Diana returning to England for Duff's first election, to be met by the Duchess (centre), and Diana's nieces, Caroline and Elizabeth Paget.

Lady Diana Duff Cooper, stage and screen star, and Society beauty, has turned politician for a time, and this week has been canvassing the voters of Oldham on her husband's behalf, he being the Conservative candidate. In our picture Lady "Di" is having a friendly chat with a number of Lancashire mill lasses in the constituency.

—Central News.

LADY "DI" TAKES OLDHAM BY STORM.

The Most Captivating Canvasser In The Country—Will She Get Her Husband To Parliament?—How She Woos The Voters In Mill-Land.

Lady Diana Duff-Cooper, the fascinating Society beauty and actress, is canvassing Oldham on behalf of her husband, Mr. A. Duff-Cooper, the Conservative candidate.

She has taken Oldham by storm.

Oldham likes the experience of being wooed for its votes by a duke's daughter. Oldham may vote Tory or it may not, but its electors will always look back to the present general election as Lady "Di's"—an enlivening experience in an appeal to the country which most other constituencies are finding incredibly dull.

She has proved the most interesting woman who has ever taken part in a ____ election, and ____

a whimsical smile. "Are you sure that no one can induce you to try?" I asked, and she replied, "If I did make a shot at it I should only make a hash of it. I simply cannot speak in public, and—well——"; which was expressively final.

Before this conversation Lady Diana had been on a visit of inspection to one of the mills in Oldham, and she was eager to talk about the "perfectly wonderful reception" all the employees gave her and her husband.

BUT THIS IS WHAT SHE SAID.

Whether Lady ____ avoided public speak-ing ____ ____ suffering from stage ____ that gave rise to much ____ respondent). "Many how a lady who has ____ ____ be ____ 'o

Her hat was a "squashed" black felt, with irregular lines.

LADY "DI'S" GRIEF.
Little Girl Knocked Down By Her Motor.

Just before ten o'clock one night she was driving from one meeting to another to meet her husband when the car knocked down Florence Widdall, aged 10, of 85, Egerton-street. The girl, along with her little brother and father, were crossing the road when the accident happened. The girl's left leg was fractured.

As soon as the accident occurred Lady Diana left the car and assisted in carrying the injured girl into her home, and re-mained there until the arrival of the am-bulance. Lady Diana, who ____ moved, did her best to ____

"I'll fight till I drop," says Lady Diana Cooper, ____ tioneering at Oldham this week to help her hu____ the Conservative candidate.

LADY DIANA'S OFFER

"If You Get My Husband In I Will Dance a Clog Dance"

Lady Diana Duff Cooper, who is assisting her husband, Mr. A. Duff Cooper, in his candidature at Oldham, has promised to dance a clog dance if her husband wins the seat.

As soon as she appeared on the platform of an Oldham meeting last night, she was handed a mysterious parcel.

Whilst her husband was speaking she investi-gated the contents and found a beautifully-finished pair of Lancashire clogs, about four inches in length, and a card bearing the inscription: "As presented to the Prince of Wales. Best wishes for your success."

When she rose to speak, Lady Diana said: "If you get my husband in at this election, I will put on a pair of clogs and dance a clog dance."

*Below: The triumphant
candidate and his wife,
October 1924.*

OLDHAM
CONSERVATIVE ASSOCIATION.

COMPLIMENTARY

Dinner and Presentation

TO

ALFRED DUFF COOPER, ESQ., D.S.O.
AND
LADY DIANA COOPER,

CENTRAL CONSERVATIVE CLUB,
OLDHAM ON FEBRUARY 26TH.
1930.

CHAIRMAN.
Councillor A. J. HOWCROFT, J.P.

Menu.

HORS D'ŒUVRES   (VARIOUS)

SOUP
TURTLE

FISH
BOILED TURBOT   LOBSTER SAUCE

REMOVES
ROAST SADDLE OF MUTTON
RED CURRANT JELLY

POULTRY
ROAST TURKEY   SAUSAGE   STUFFING
BREAD SAUCE

BAKED AND BOILED POTATOES
VEGETABLES IN SEASON

SWEETS
APPLE TART AND CREAM

SAVOURY
DESSERT   COFFEE

Celebrities abroad

Three visitors from England join forces in Berlin. Lady Diana Cooper, Arnold Bennett and Mrs. Montagu

LADY DIANA COOPER

Right: Oswald Mosley (Tom), whom Duff described as an 'adulterous, canting, slimy, slobbering Bolshie.' His opinion did not improve when Mosley's politics moved to the Right.

Touring in the Sahara, 1928, with the Ednams. (Above) Clare Sheridan mounted on an Arab stallion. (Right) Rosemary Ednam (later Countess of Dudley) and Duff in the desert near Biskra; below, Diana and Duff.

The Bahamas: Diana with the
shark she caught, and on the
beach with Duff, Michael
Herbert and Biddy Carlisle.

Above: Diana near Lake Louise, when staying with Duff at the E.P. Ranch, the Prince of Wales's property in Alberta, Canada.

7
FRIENDS AND POLITICS
1928–1939

*M*rs Algernon Stitch is Diana's most famous appearance in fiction, and the character closely follows the original. Evelyn Waugh met Diana in 1932 during the English revival of *The Miracle*, and fell under her spell. By then over forty, Diana's beauty had scarcely diminished, due to the fine bone structure of her face. She was eccentric, and as heedless of convention as she was of the highway code — a trait for which Mrs Stitch was also famous.

'*The Miracle* always brought me good things,' said Diana, for about the same time as it introduced Evelyn Waugh into her life, it also brought her Conrad Russell. This tall, humorous, tranquil man, whose life was devoted to books, farming and writing letters, became one of the firmest rocks in her agitated life; and unlike Waugh, Conrad never tried to seduce her.

Both men visited Bognor frequently as did other writers like Hilaire Belloc, Maurice Baring, A. E. W. Mason, and Arnold Bennett. Pebble-dashed, with a verandah and Gothic windows on the ground floor, the cottage looked on to a garden protected by a high wall beyond which was the beach. Whenever possible, Diana preferred to eat outside. Rex Whistler and Cecil Beaton, or political colleagues like Winston Churchill and Brendan Bracken, would gather round her lunch table; and on particularly fine days, the whole party would set off to picnic on Halnaker Hill — an outing particularly favoured by John Julius.

Until Duff's promotion from Minister of War to First Lord of the Admiralty in 1937, No. 90 Gower street was their London home. From there, they would often part company for the evening. Duff was a gregarious clubman and, while he dined and played cards with his cronies at White's, Diana might be seen at any of a dozen places; with Chips Channon, Max Beaverbrook or Emerald Cunard, or at the theatre with her favourite escorts, 'The Boys': the barrister St. John Hutchinson, and the ever-faithful Alan Parsons, until his early death in 1936.

The Gower Street parties continued. One of the most exciting was held on the night of the General Election in October 1931, with a wireless in every room to broadcast the incoming results. Among the throng that drove back and forth between Bloomsbury and Westminster was Winston Churchill, who wept when he heard that his son Randolph had been defeated.

Another guest that night was the Prince of Wales, whom Diana and Duff had seen from time to time since those days of the Duchess's fond hopes of a great match. Later, during his relationship with Wallis Simpson, he enjoyed the company of the Coopers and often invited them for weekends at Fort Belvedere. These were very luxurious and often fun, but Duff and Diana never really liked Wallis Simpson and remained firm friends with some of the Prince's old favourites, like Freda Dudley Ward and Thelma Furness. For the Prince, who was so obviously in Wallis's thrall, they continued to feel a sad loyalty.

In the summer of 1936, Duff and Diana accompanied the new King on his Mediterranean cruise aboard the yacht *Nahlin*. In the story of the Abdication, these six weeks marked a crucial development. For the King to have a mistress was one thing; but to make her the hostess on board his

M. Duff-Cooper, ministre anglais de la Guerre

Previous page: Lunch in the garden at Bognor, with A. E. W. Mason, Barbara and Victor Rothschild, Kaetchen Kommer, Duff and Daisy Fellowes.

yacht, and to put in at foreign ports expecting them both to be treated like royalty, was quite another. Diana felt that Wallis was rather bored by the King's obsessive attentions, and his habit of apologising for everything, from the food to the company.

In 1937 Duff was promoted to First Lord of the Admiralty. Diana was delighted with Admiralty House, though sad to leave Gower Street. The job also brought with it the use of the steam yacht *HMS Enchantress*, and they took ample advantage of this opportunity to mix official duties with pleasure. Their first journey in the *Enchantress* started in Venice and took them to the Eastern Mediterranean. In the summer of 1938, accompanied by George and Imogen Gage and Diana's niece Elizabeth Paget, Duff and Diana sailed to the Baltic.

It was in Danzig, at a shooting party organised in Duff's honour, that Diana met Carl Burckhardt, the League of Nations High Commissioner. They were immediately attracted to one another. 'What would you say if Lady Weymouth and I carried on like that?' complained Conrad Russell; but Duff, it seemed, could never be made jealous.

The Baltic cruise was brought to a dramatic end by a radio message announcing an urgent Cabinet meeting to discuss the Czechoslovakian crisis. When Duff stepped off the *Enchantress* in London, he did not know it was for the last time.

AT SUNNY BOGNOR. 1929

THE sunshine and the heat tempted me to seek the sea breeze at Bognor for a few brief hours.

As I walked near Aldwick—which, as you know is just an extension of Bognor—I saw a speedy Chrysler gliding along the corkscrew lanes. At the wheel was Lady Diana Cooper, her husband sitting by her side.

Very well and happy I thought Lady Diana looked as I caught this fleeting glimpse of her.

LADY DUFF COOPER IN RED SLACKS

Court Fine Sequel to Motoring Offence

Wearing a large Mexican hat and red slacks, Lady Diana Olive Maud Duff Cooper, wife of the Minister of Information, who lives at Aldwick, near Bognor Regis, was fined a total of 25s. with 5s. costs at Bognor Regis yesterday for causing an obstuction with a motor car, driving without a licence and failing to immobilise her car.

She pleaded guilty to the first two summonses but not guilty to the third.

P.c. Hunt said that the ignition key was still in position. There was a dog in the car, but he was able to get in and take the key.

Lady Duff Cooper told the magistrates that she was collecting swill for pigs. She could not park on the proper side of the road because she could not reverse with the trailer

Asked why she had not immobilised the car she pointed out that she had a dog in the car and added: "The dog is really a guard but I suppose he recognised a policeman."

Lady Diana Was In a Hurry— Pays £3 Fine

LADY DIANA COOPER, whose address was given as Gower-street, London, W., was fined £3 and her licence endorsed at Horsham to-day for speeding at Five Oaks, near Horsham, on June 20.

P.-c. Scotcher gave her speed as 47 to 61 m.p.h.

Mr. P. G. Eager, who represented Lady Diana, and pleaded guilty, explained that she was in a hurry as she had the First Lord of the Admiralty in her car.

The Clerk of the Court.—"Was he hurrying to resign?"

Above: Diana's piratical driving was notorious, and Evelyn Waugh used it to memorable effect in his portrait of her as Mrs. Algernon Stitch in 'Scoop': 'She mounted the kerb and bowled rapidly along the pavement to the corner of St. James's, where a policeman took her number and ordered her into the road. "Third time this week," said Mrs. Stitch. "I wish they wouldn't. It's such a nuisance for Algy."'

Right: Evelyn Waugh in Abyssinia, in his lion-skin coat: a photograph he gave Diana.

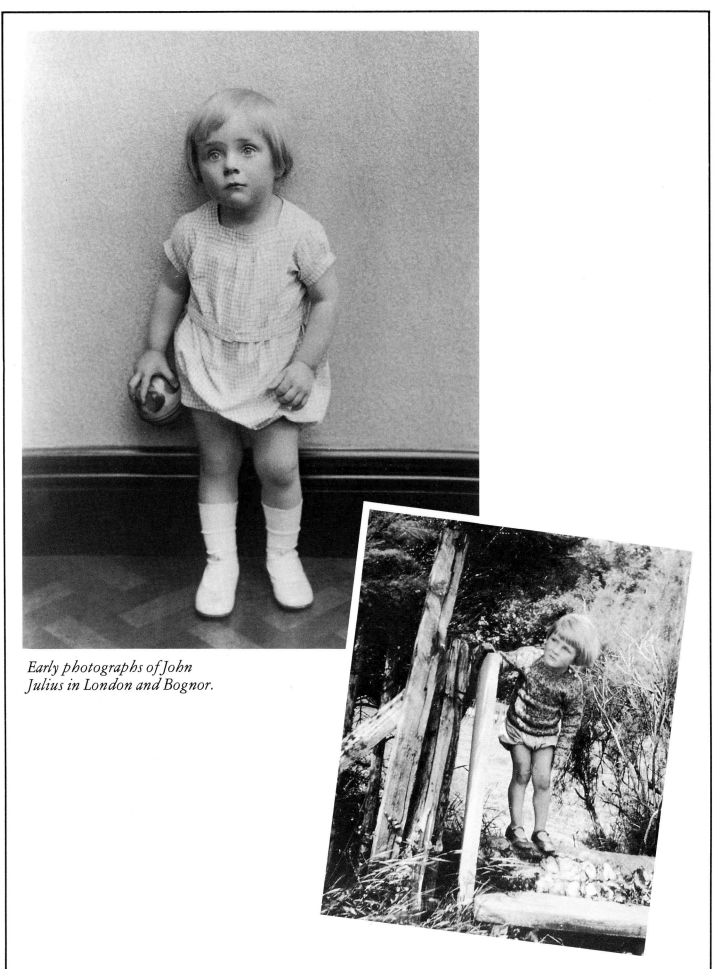

Early photographs of John Julius in London and Bognor.

Summers at Bognor: Arnold Bennett about to lose his hat and A. E. W. Mason thinking.

Right: Rex Whistler in Diana's hat working on his watercolour of West House, watched by John Julius, and (above) the finished painting.

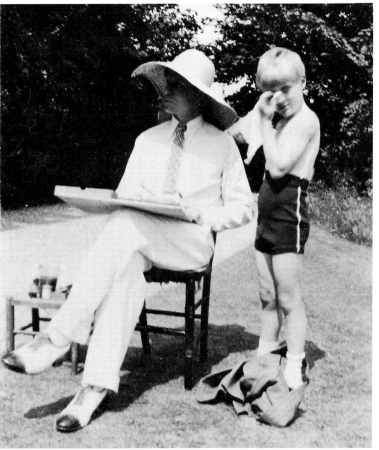

Above: Duff, Diana, Daisy
Fellowes, Barbara and Victor
Rothschild.

Left: Doris Castlerosse and
Maurice Baring.

Opposite top: Brendan
Bracken.

Opposite bottom: Diana and
Duff in the garden at Bognor,
with his study in the
background.

Above: At the theatre with the barrister St. John Hutchinson.

Right: Cecil Beaton's drawing of Daisy Fellowes, reputedly one of the best dressed women in the world.

Daisy Fellowes 1934

Above: A sketch of Duff on the
back of a menu by Sir Edwin Lutyens.

Above: Winston and Clementine Churchill.

Right: On a cruise to Brazil, as the guest of Lord Beaverbrook, seen with Frank Owen and Valentine Castlerosse, the Daily Express gossip columnist.

Opposite top: The Minister of War leaving Gower Street.

Gower St. _him for War?_

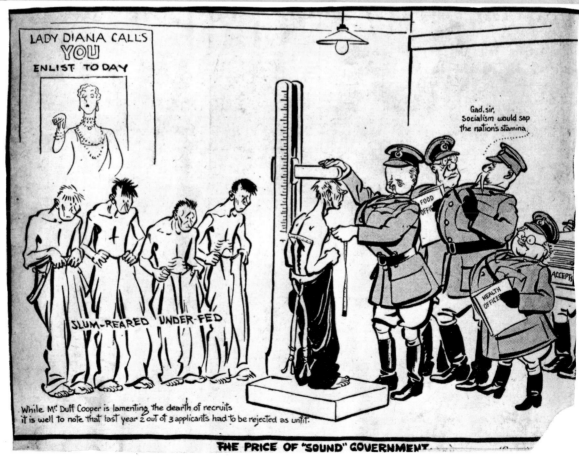

Opposite top: The King smoking a pipe, with Diana and Wallis Simpson at Aegina.

Opposite bottom: Returning to the 'Nahlin': the King, following Wallis Simpson and Diana.

Above: The cruise of the 'Nahlin' in the Adriatic, August 1936. King Edward VIII and Helen Fitzgerald on board, with a jigsaw puzzle of a glamour girl.

TONY WYSARD'S WAXWORKS

EXHIBIT 2

THE Rt Hon A. AND LADY DIANA. DUFF COOPER

THE FIRST LORD OF THE ADMIRALTY AND HIS WIFE

HEAD WORK BY DUFF COOPER

Excitement runs high among the natives on the Mediterranean about the unusual hat worn by our visiting First Lord of Admiralty, the report having got around that it was a new type of defence against air attack. British prestige is rising

For Duff and Diana, one of the great pleasures of his appointment as First Lord of the Admiralty was the yacht HMS 'Enchantress', seen here anchored off Venice. 'She was a sloop with a crew of 150 captained by Peter Frend, with her stern converted into living quarters for the First Lord, his wife and four friends. She had two big saloons, and later another superstructure was added for Duff to work in. The officers knew this as the Duff Cot.'

Top: Duff faced with a Nazi salute, at the shoot organised in his honour near Danzig. Left: This photograph of Duff, less correctly dressed than usual, was Diana's favourite. Above right: Carl Burckhardt, 'this glorious Swiss', in a photograph he gave to Diana.

Opposite: On a picnic near Kiel: Liz Paget standing, Imogen Gage (sister of Julian Grenfell), Admiral Troubridge and Diana. Right: Duff with Liz Paget at Bognor, shortly before her marriage to Raimund von Hofmannsthal, far right.

Above: A picnic on Halnaker Hill — the subject of a poem by Hilaire Belloc — with Duff, Diana, John Julius and members of the Wallace family, just before the outbreak of war.

8
THE SECOND WORLD WAR
1939–1944

*B*y the time they reached Hollywood, to stay with Jack Warner on the last leg of Duff's American lecture tour, Diana's depression had lifted. Although initially intimidated by the 'up-to-the-markishness' of it all, she soon relaxed enough to enjoy the parties and small lunches organised for them by their hosts. As a result, they met Douglas Fairbanks Jr., David Selznick, Charlie Chaplin, Marlene Dietrich and Vivien Leigh.

After such luxury and grandeur, the austerity measures at home had a slightly disorienting effect. Diana threw herself into war work, waiting for Duff to be given office. But during his unhappy time as Minister of Information, she found she could do little to help him in London, so in April 1941 she moved down to Bognor. There, with the assistance of Miss Wade, who had been her maid for over twenty years, Diana turned the cottage and its land into a small-holding. Undaunted by her ignorance of the subject, she consulted the relevant books and sought the help of Conrad Russell. Between his visits they wrote each other long letters, devoted mostly to animal husbandry and cheese making, but with plenty of room for recipes, books and gossip.

Diana was visited by friends from London who wanted to escape the Blitz, including Emerald Cunard, and Cecil Beaton who photographed her at work. Few could credit her transformation from *grande dame* to smallholder: 'To think', wrote Chips Channon, 'the world's most beautiful woman showing off her swill.' But Diana loved her rural existence, with its hard work and relative tranquility.

Diana insisted on accompanying Duff on his mission to Singapore, but she was at work on the smallholding soon after they got back in the spring of 1942. Her greatest joy at this time was John Julius's return from Canada. For a few days she had him to herself at Bognor, before he left to begin his first half at Eton.

Duff meanwhile remained as Chancellor of the Duchy of Lancaster. His main task was to deal with aspects of secret warfare, a subject close to the heart of the Prime Minister. During a 'bomber moon', Churchill would often stay at Ditchley Park, the home of Ronald Tree and his wife. Duff and Diana were sometimes in the party, and she described the country's leader in her inimitable style:

> Winston dresses night and day, and I imagine in bed, in the same blue workman's boiler suit. He looks exactly like the good little pig building his house with bricks. On his feet he bears inappropriately a pair of gold-embroidered black slippers that I gave him — more suited to the silk-stockinged leg of William Pitt.

When they left for Algiers in January 1944, Duff was full of optimism. At last he had a job that was satisfying, and looked forward to becoming ambassador in Paris after the liberation. Diana was miserable at leaving Bognor again, and her first impressions only seemed to confirm her dejection. But she soon overcame the disadvantages of their unpromising quarters and made their life 'wonderfully unambassadorial', with parrots, a tame gazelle and a cow to compensate for the loss of Bognor.

The stream of friends seemed endless. Virginia Cowles brought a fellow

Previous page: Diana making cheese at Bognor, photographed by Cecil Beaton.

journalist, Martha Gellhorn, who became another life-long friend. Victor Rothschild stayed with them, as did Evelyn Waugh and Randolph Churchill. Diana also entertained the Prime Minister and his wife, both officially and informally. Lord Moran, Churchill's personal physician, observed that she was 'one of the few women who is not intimidated by Winston'.

The politician she really came to admire at this time was Harold Macmillan, the Minister Resident. 'He's a splendid man,' she wrote. 'One day he'll be Prime Minister. I've put my money (nay, my shirt) on him.' Among the French, Diana particularly liked André Gide and General de Lattre de Tassigny, of whom she wrote. 'He is a romantic figure. One pictures him with Flemish lace laid on his armour. Such intrepid gallantry, such bold effeminacy.'

When Paris was liberated, Diana could not bear the thought of leaving Algiers, and dreaded the serious formality that awaited her as *Madame l'ambassadrice*.

Right: Diana, Jack Warner, Duff and Douglas Fairbanks Jr. in Hollywood, February 1940.

Opposite: The former Minister of War reverts to his old uniform.

Left: Conrad Russell with bayonet fixed.

Below: Conrad Russell and Daphne Weymouth, his other favourite companion and correspondent.

Above: George Gordon Moore, Diana's admirer from the First World War, Kaetchen Kommer, and John Julius at the top of the Empire State Building in New York.

Opposite: Cecil Beaton photographing Diana milking Princess, on the Bognor smallholding.

The curtain falls on Michael Redgrave thus in act I of THUNDER ROCK.

Lights up reveal Lady Diana Cooper in the audience.

Right: Cartoon of Diana at the theatre, when Duff was Minister of Information.

Above and left: Cecil Beaton's photographs of Emerald Cunard's visit to Bognor: Diana described her reactions. 'Oh, Diana, this is very interesting! How do you do it? These are your pigs? Very interesting pigs! How can you milk that cow?'

Above: A weekend with the Queensberrys, before leaving for Singapore. Lord Alfred Douglas, Duff, Lady Queensberry, Edward Stanley, Diana, Lady Mappin, Francis Queensberry. Diana remembered how they had resigned themselves to a tactful silence on the subject of Oscar Wilde, only to find that Lord Alfred Douglas would talk of nothing else.

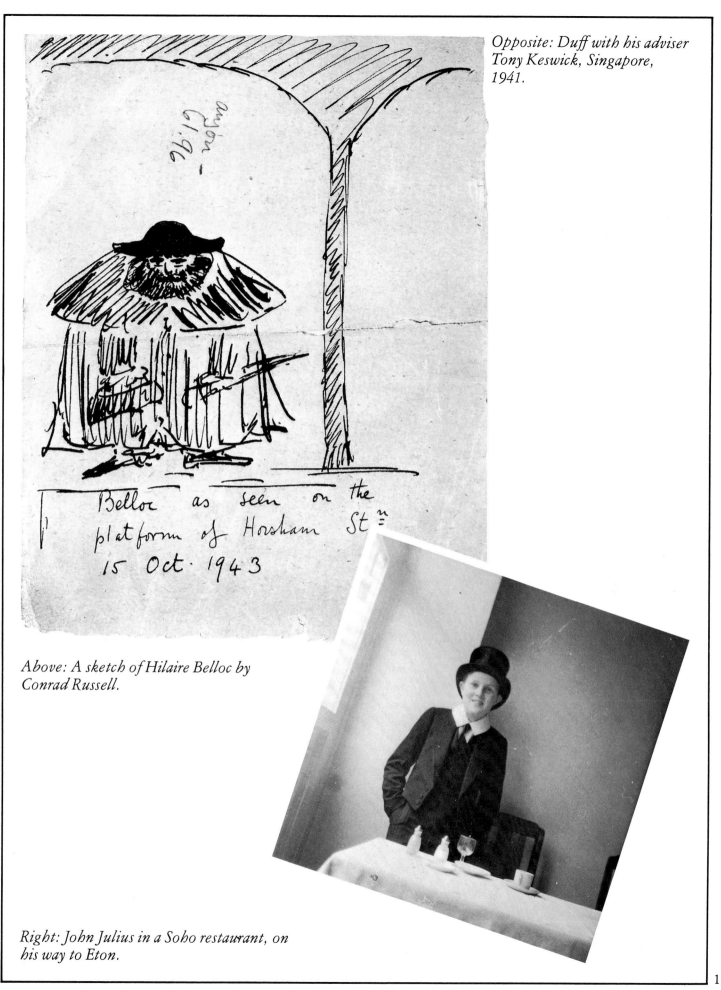

Opposite: Duff with his adviser Tony Keswick, Singapore, 1941.

Bellon — 9.1.6

Belloc as seen on the platform of Horsham Stⁿ

15 Oct. 1943

Above: A sketch of Hilaire Belloc by Conrad Russell.

Right: John Julius in a Soho restaurant, on his way to Eton.

Above: Winston Churchill and Duff at Ditchley.

Left: Rex Whistler in the uniform of the Welsh Guards not long before his death in Normandy.

Opposite top: Lunch in Algiers with Teddie Phillips out of uniform, Commander George Fitzgeorge in uniform and Duff preoccupied with local diplomacy.

Opposite bottom: Victor Rothschild and Duff.

Overleaf: Pamela Berry, later Lady Hartwell, and Diana in Dorchester days.

137

9
PARIS
1944–1947

*O*nce again, the Coopers arrived to improvisation and chaos, unlike most ambassadors taking up a new appointment. In September 1944, the British Embassy was suffering from five years of neglect and accumulated junk. They lived in a hotel while Diana set to work clearing the house, which had to be presentable to receive Winston Churchill for the first post-war reception on November 11.

In January 1945, Diana was invited to the front in her role of regimental godmother to the *1er Chasseurs d'Afrique*. She arranged for John Julius, on holiday from school, to be included; and General de Lattre, the French C-in-C, took them across the Rhine and arranged a tour of his section of the front. De Lattre ordered a guard of honour for her to inspect. 'This was very embarrassing,' Diana wrote to Conrad afterwards,

> as I had no idea how to do it. Duckling [her nickname for Churchill] once told me he looked every man full in the eyes. I tried, but no eye would meet mine. One feels one ought to say 'Bravo' or 'Well dressed, sir'.

Although she performed the good works and entertaining expected of an ambassadress, Diana had difficulty settling into her life in Paris, and initially she was tormented by anxiety and lack of sleep. Once the first miserable months were over, however, her character began to reassert itself. The brittle dignity of the French was frequently offended by her disregard for protocol and precedence — but more disturbing were the rumours of collaborators among her guests.

Diana attracted a group of intimates wherever she stayed, and in Paris they were known as *la Bande*. Many of its members were artists, who at that time seemed particularly vulnerable to accusations of collaboration. Diana defended them all stoutly. She argued that if any of them were damaging the Embassy's reputation, then her friend Gaston Palewski, de Gaulle's *chef de cabinet*, would be the first to warn her.

The tone of *la Bande* was high spirited and Bohemian. It included the composer Georges Auric, the pianist Jacques Février, the painter Drian, the director of the *Comédie Française* Edouard Bourdet and his wife, Christian Bérard the stage designer, and Jean Cocteau. Cocteau had found a place in Diana's circle thanks to Cecil Beaton, who often stayed at the Embassy during the next few years. He and Bérard helped her restore the house in the style of its most famous occupant, Napoleon's sister Pauline Borghese. Others associated with the group were the choreographer Serge Lifar, and the industrialist patron of the arts Paul-Louis Weiller, soon to be decorated with the Médaille de la Résistance.

One member in particular had a major effect on both Duff and Diana's life. This was the writer Louise de Vilmorin. 'The British Embassy gets stranger and stranger', wrote Susan Mary Patten:

> Imagine Evelyn Waugh, Lord Carlisle, the Bishop of Fulham, Harold Laski, and Peter Quennell all under one roof and none of them loath to speak up at the table, and all outdone by Louise de Vilmorin, who got fed up at not being allowed to tell a story, so she threw her butter ball up to the ceiling with her butter knife. It held there, stronger than the planet Venus, and so mesmerizing was this feat that all conversation stopped, permitting Louise to launch into one of her truly spellbinding tales.

Previous page: Jean Cocteau's drawing of a unicorn for Diana, 1946.

Louise suffered most from the snake-pit of suspicion which Paris had become after the occupation, with people trying to hide their own complicity by denouncing others. In her case the whispers were based on a confusion of names. And when Duff was told that Louise's presence provoked disapproval, he flew into one of his most violent rages. Both he and Diana thought her the most brilliant and bewitching woman they had ever met. Diana, whose tolerance of Duff's infidelities was already legendary, genuinely approved of their affair; and when Duff's passion cooled, it was she who consoled the distraught Lulu.

In September 1945, Duff and Diana helped the Duke and Duchess of Windsor on their return to France. The Duke, lonely and bored, sought the company of Duff, who reflected on how pathetic his existence must be, sharing 'an apartment on the third floor of the Ritz with that harsh-voiced ageing woman who was never even pretty.' Diana was even less fond of Wallis and dreaded their parties. But loyalty to the ex-King as well as gratitude for past hospitality at Fort Belvedere, on the *Nahlin* and at the EP Ranch in Canada, prompted her to include them in several Embassy dinners. One of these parties became rather heavy going when Noël Coward and the Duke tried to out-do each other with naval reminiscences, the Duke's based on his time at Dartmouth and in the Bahamas, and Coward's on his experiences preparing the film *In Which We Serve*.

When the Labour government came to power at the end of the war, Duff knew that his Paris days must be numbered. However great Ernie Bevin's respect for Duff and fascination for Diana, a prominent Conservative simply could not be kept on indefinitely.

By the time the fateful letter came in September, Duff was prepared. The Treaty of Dunkirk had fulfilled his ambitions. Now, he looked forward to his retirement and the time it offered to read and write. Diana, on the other hand, went into one of her worst depressions, haunted by visions of old age and a bleak future.

Winston S. Churchill *C. de Gaulle*

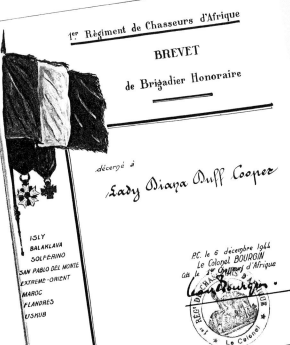

Above: Winston Churchill and General de Gaulle, in Paris on Armistice Day 1944.

Left: Diana's appointment as 'Godmother' to the 1er Chasseurs d'Afrique. In this capacity she and John Julius were taken on a tour of the front by General de Lattre de Tassigny, a friend from Algiers.

Left: General de Lattre de Tassigny, John Julius in Eton cadet uniform, and Diana — in her own words — 'looking awful in a tartan coat and postman's cap'.

Below: Diana trying to follow Churchill's advice to look a guard of honour in the eyes: 'I tried, but no eye would meet mine. One feels one ought to say "Bravo" or "well dressed, sir".'

143

Left: Winston Churchill in Paris; and on another visit (below), with Venetia Montagu and Clementine on the steps of the Embassy.

Opposite: A children's tea party at the Embassy.

Opposite: After dinner conversation at the Embassy: Léon Blum, Vincent Auriol, Winston Churchill, and Georges Bidault.

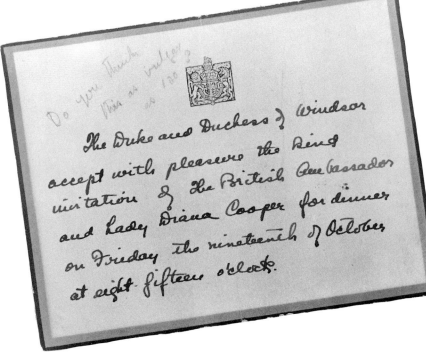

Top: Gerald van der Kemp,
Jean-Denis Maillard,
unidentified, Diana Cooper,
Paul-Louis Weiller, Edmonde
Charles-Roux, Aliette Gilet,
Serge Lifar, Nora Auric.

Left: The Duchess of Windsor's
stationery, bordered in two
tones of blue, fails to gain
Diana's approval.

Left: Diana and Paul-Louis Weiller.

Below: A ballet by Serge Lifar in honour of Diana (seated centre) staged in the garden of the Embassy.

Mon corps, mon âme, mon portrait.
A Diana   Louise.

Left: A self-portrait of Louise de Vilmorin,
and a photograph (below) by Cecil Beaton
in the British Embassy with her pug Bijou.

Bottom: Duff and Susan Mary Patten.

Above: Duff being made Chevalier du Taste-vin, and (right) with Marie-Laure de Noailles.

Opposite: The ambassador in evening dress.

Above: The signing of the Treaty of Dunkirk, by Georges Bidault and Ernest Bevin, in 1947.

Above: Diana on Pauline Borghese's bed in the British Embassy; photograph by Cecil Beaton.

10
CHANTILLY
1946–1960

$\mathcal{W}$hile exploring the woods that surround the Château de Chantilly, Diana had come across a beautiful house, with lawns sloping down to an ornamental lake.

> I walked through open iron gates (an ingrained and irresistible habit) to an eighteenth-century house clearly built for the retirement of a scholarly English lover of life and his doting wife.

Diana discovered that it belonged to the Institut de France, and negotiations for a lease were in hand well before their departure from the Embassy.

In Nancy Mitford's novel *Don't Tell Alfred*, an incoming ambassadress to Paris notices that while several distinguished people enter the Embassy courtyard, they never appear in her drawing room. She discovers that her beautiful predecessor — a character based on Diana — refuses to move out, and is holding court in an unused wing of the house. Diana was not quite that tenacious, but she made no secret of her feeling that Duff had been pushed out of the Embassy before his time. As far as she was concerned, the new ambassador Sir Oliver Harvey and his wife were usurpers, and she had no qualms about embarrassing them with her continued presence in France.

Although *la Bande* had dispersed on Diana's departure from the Faubourg Saint-Honoré, a new combination of friends collected around her at Chantilly. Those based in Paris, like Nancy Mitford, Louise de Vilmorin, and François Valéry, would come for long Sunday lunches on the terrace overlooking the lake. They would be joined by a continual stream of visitors from England, staying at the house or passing through Paris. Chantilly's relaxed assortment of writers, politicians, musicians and royalty was typical of Diana's entertaining. The Arcadian beauty of the surroundings inspired her. Sometimes Diana would take her guests for a walk in the woods and 'discover' a magnificent picnic in some unexpected place. And 'Sometimes,' as Susan Mary wrote,

> the picnics were at night, and we would find ourselves led (the surprise element was part of the charm) through the forest to a fairy tale building called the Pavilion of the White Queen which lies beside a lake. At the water's edge a table was laid on a little landing stage, candlelit and formal with Diana's best china. As the moon came up over the towers of Chantilly Castle across the water someone, probably John Julius, began to play French ballads on the guitar.

There was something enchanted about Diana's world, and her guests were delighted to enter it with her.

John Julius, having completed his national service in the Navy, went up to Oxford to read Russian and French. He met Anne Clifford while still at New College, and their wedding took place soon after his final exams. Diana admired her daughter-in-law's beauty and strong, artistic nature, but disapproved of their marrying so young, with John Julius just embarking on a career in the Foreign Office. Their first child, born a year later, was called Artemis, in honour of her grandmother; and Diana later took as much trouble over her education as she had for John Julius.

Duff enjoyed his last few years of writing and reflection, before his death in 1954 at the age of sixty-three. For many months Diana could not bring herself to go back to the house they had loved so much. When she did return, the lunches and the weekend parties began again, but the best days of Chantilly were over. Diana always hoped that John Julius would be posted to the Paris Embassy so life could continue as before. But over the next few years, he was sent first to Belgrade, and subsequently to Beirut — where Diana's second grandchild, Jason, was born in 1959.

Diana could have renewed the lease on the Château de Saint-Firmin, but there seemed no reason to do so when John Julius was posted back to London in the following year.

Right: The drawing room at the Château de Saint-Firmin, Chantilly.

Left: Marina, Duchess of Kent at Chantilly, photograph by Cecil Beaton.

Bottom left: Rachel and David Cecil.

Below: François Valéry, John Julius and Nancy Mitford, with the house in the background.

Left: A bust of Diana by Reid Dick.

Below: Evelyn Waugh at Chantilly.

Left: Duff with his spaniel Willow.

Above: August 5th, 1952. Duff and Diana arrive for John Julius's wedding at Sutton Place, which then belonged to the Duke of Sutherland.

Above: John Julius and the three Clifford sisters: Pandora, Anne, Atalanta, and in the foreground, Pandora's daughter Annabel Jones.

Above: Duff with Diana's niece Caroline, at Opio, Grasse.

Left: On the bridge in the park of Chantilly: Raimund von Hofmannsthal, Totor de Lesseps, Richard Faber, Princess Maria Pia of Yugoslavia, Philip Ziegler, Maurice Bowra, Anne, Amabel Lindsay, Patrick Lindsay, Judy Montagu, Prince Alexander of Yugoslavia.

Opposite: Duff signing copies of Louise de Vilmorin's translation of his novel, 'Operation Heartbreak'.

Right: Lunch on the terrace at Chantilly: Dorothy (Dot) Head, and in the background John Julius, Patrick Kinross, Antony Head, Hugh Fraser, and Diana's future biographer Philip Ziegler.

Right: John Julius and Diana on the terrace steps.

Above: John Julius, Artemis and Anne in their house in Beirut.

Right: Artemis picking cyclamen by the Dog River in Lebanon.

11
TRAVELS AND DISTRACTIONS
1948–1960

$\mathcal{I}$n a letter to Diana written in
1926, Duff told Diana that 'Clemmie [Churchill] said she didn't think you
would like Corsica because it is very wild and the hotel would be very
simple and primitive, which is of course just what you do like, poor freak,
isn't it'. Duff could never understand her yearning for adventure, nor she
his attachment to comfort; yet in the last years of his life, they were both
content with old haunts: Paris, San Vigilio, Venice, and the South of
France.

A holiday with Diana was never without incident, even when she had
not planned it. At Monte Carlo, on their return from visiting Daisy
Fellowes on her yacht, they found a crowd gathered to watch their car being
hauled out of the harbour. Duff blamed drunken sailors; but Diana told
the press it was Communists, out for her husband's blood.

A happier experience awaited them in Venice in 1951, when Charles de
Beistegui gave a ball on a scale the city had not seen since the eighteenth
century. Dressed as Tiepolo's Cleopatra, who adorns the walls of the
Palazzo Labia, Diana sat enthroned to receive the salutations of the guests
as they made their magnificent entries. Only a few hours before, Oliver
Messel and Cecil Beaton — usually implacable rivals — had been sewing
her into the costume they had designed after Tiepolo; while she sewed a
bag for Duff's hip-flask, because his domino lacked pockets.

Duff was the first to admit that in the course of his life he had consist-
ently drunk more than was good for him, and did not complain when his
health began to deteriorate. In the spring of 1953, he became extremely ill.
He bore everything cheerfully, except the plain diet, and insisted that
Diana go to the Coronation without him. In December, they set off to
spend the winter in Jamaica. Duff was suddenly taken ill on board ship,
and died on New Year's Day, 1954.

After his burial at Belvoir, Diana collapsed into a seemingly bottomless
depression. To escape the memories of Chantilly, she travelled restlessly
from one place to another, accompanied by a succession of friends. Her
journeys that year to Spain and Morocco were followed by another to
Tuscany, Rome and Greece. Two months in Chantilly with an overgrown
garden and problems about her tenancy drove her to England, and from
house to house that she had known in the past with Duff.

On her return from another visit to Africa in 1955, Stavros Niarchos
promised her the use of his yacht, the *Creole*, to cruise the Mediterranean.
A more regular feature of her summers were visits to La Reine Jeanne, the
beautiful villa of Paul-Louis Weiller in the south of France.

When memories became less painful she went back to Chantilly, but the
travelling continued. Over the next few years, her alternative base was
Rome, where she stayed with Iris Tree, or Judy Montagu, who was later to
marry Milton Gendel. She loved to hear Milton call her 'Gaadess' in his
American accent; and with him and Judy, Patrick and Jenny Crosse and the
painter Derek Hill, then head of the British Institute, she would plan
picnics and excursions into the Campagna.

The other focus of her travels was John Julius, attached first to the British
Embassy in Yugoslavia, and then in Lebanon. With him and Anne, she

*Previous page: Diana in the
Valley of the Kings,
photographed by John Julius
on the following donkey.*

164

Below: The marriage of Caroline Paget and Michael Duff, 1949. Standing: Mickey Renshaw, David Herbert, Liz von Hofmannsthal, Michael Duff, Duff, Diana, and Raimund. Sitting: Juliet Duff (Michael's mother), Caroline with Liz's children, Arabella and Octavian, and Cecil Beaton.

visited Jordan and Egypt, using Beirut as a base, and returned to listen to the traveller's tales told by Freya Stark and Christopher Scaife in his beautiful house at Ain Anoub.

With time on her hands, Diana gave in to the urgings of Rupert Hart-Davis, Duff's nephew, to write her autobiography. Despite a morbid lack of confidence, the first volume — *The Rainbow Comes and Goes* — was published in 1958. To her astonishment, the book was a critical and commercial success. She wrote two more volumes, *The Light of Common Day* and *Trumpets from the Steep*, before moving back to London.

Above: San Vigilio, on Lake Garda.

John Julius and Liz.

'We went down a cypress-
sentinelled hill to a point of
land silver with olives, and
there was an inn, once no
doubt a cloistered house, with
room in its stone port to hold
one fishing boat . . . from that
day until 1953, hardly a year of
peace-time passed without a
week or more of heart's content
at San Vigilio.'

Below: 'After my car slipped into the sea at Monte Carlo'.
Diana surveys the damage.

Left: Duff, Diana and Liz, Lake Garda.

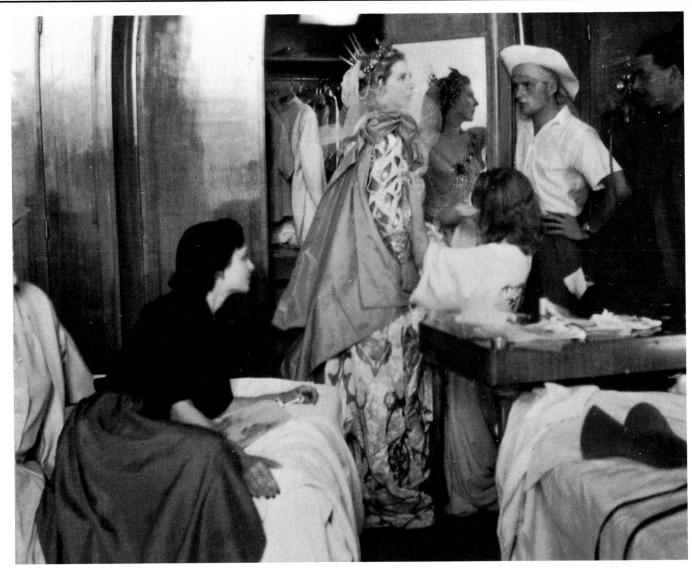

*The Beistegui Ball, Venice,
1951. Diana being dressed as
Tiepolo's Cleopatra in the
Gritti Hotel, with Liz von
Hofmannsthal, Anne, John
Julius, and Oliver Messel.
Left: John Julius and Liz.*

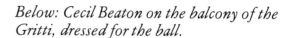

Their host, Charles de Beistegui, dressed as a Venetian Procurator in the Palazzo Labia, photograph by Cecil Beaton.

Below: Cecil Beaton on the balcony of the Gritti, dressed for the ball.

Left: Daisy Fellowes as America in the Palazzo Labia, in front of one of the Tiepolo paintings of Cleopatra; photograph by Cecil Beaton.

Rome: Iris Tree on her roof garden, and below, a dinner with Judy Montagu, Patrick Crosse, Diana, Milton Gendel, and Jenny Crosse.

Left: With Stavros Niarchos on board the 'Creole'.

Below: Diana, Bernard Berenson, Nicky Mariano, and Paddy Leigh Fermor near I Tatti.

Left: With Paddy Leigh Fermor, Delos.

Left: At Paul-Louis Weiller's villa La Reine Jeanne in the South of France. On the right hand side of the table can be seen Diana, Paul-Louis, Merle Oberon, and Claus von Bülow closest to the camera.

Below: Diana and Otto Preminger at La Reine Jeanne, during the filming of 'Bonjour Tristesse'.

Christopher Scaife's house, Ain Anoub, Lebanon. Diana with Freya Stark and John Julius, and below, with John Julius and Anne.

Left: Diana and John Julius praying for release in Trogir, Yugoslavia.

*Above: Serge Lifar, Cecil Beaton and Diana at Diaghilev's tomb,
on the island of San Michele, Venice.*

Above: Signing copies of 'The Light of Common Day', in W. H. Smith's, Paris: grouped around the roses are Hoytie Wyborg, Nancy Mitford, and Count Mogens Tvede.

12
LITTLE VENICE
1960–1986

*D*iana's last home was No. 10 Warwick Avenue, just around the corner from John Julius and Anne. The bedroom was done up just as it had been at Chantilly, with a large canopied bed hung in white muslin and lace. Here she worked for most of the morning; while magazines, bills, letters, address book, cheque book, engagement book, and a telephone all fought for space with the latest biographies, some saleroom catalogues, the newspapers, the Oxford Book of English Verse, and a chihuahua called Doggie.

Diana had not lost her need to be at the heart of things, and at Warwick Avenue she entertained as wide a cross-section of London life as she could. These included old friends like Ali Forbes and Ann Fleming, as well as new ones, from the unfamiliar world of television. David Frost was a frequent guest at her Thursday lunches, as were Jim Mossman and Nigel Ryan. Nigel was her 'last attachment', and proved that Diana's gift for friendship never dimmed.

Most years took her to the Hofmannsthals in Austria, and Paul-Louis Weiller in France. There were occasional visits to Noël Coward in Switzerland, and sometimes more ambitious journeys, including Kenya and Ethiopia. A visit to America was planned by Susan Mary, now married to the columnist Joe Alsop. Diana woke to find herself the toast of Washington, following a dinner with President Kennedy, which left him shaking his head and saying, 'What a woman!'

Where once she had the Coterie and *la Bande*, Diana now had the Neighbours. Little Venice was a village; and Lennox and Freda Berkeley, Patrick Kinross, Frank and Kitty Giles, Anne and John Julius and her grandchildren were welcome to drop in whenever they felt like it. Artemis and Jason were a constant source of vexation and delight. She never ceased to complain about the idiocy of the school curriculum, and there were frequent expeditions to the zoo, the movies, and — Diana's favourite — the Planetarium.

Right into old age, her entry into a room caused heads to turn; but more and more time was spent in bed, with Doggie for company. Friends and family came in the evenings, and every weekend for years she was welcomed to the house of Charles and Kitty Farrell, her niece.

On weekdays, she received actors, research students, biographers, journalists and television producers, who came to interview her about her life and the people she had known. 'I feel older than the Sphinx,' she said. 'I'm a historic monument.' One of her interviewers was brave enough to ask her why she had become so famous. She said she had no idea. 'I've had a marvellous life, but I've never done anything very grand or remarkable. If I had to rename my autobiographies, I'd call them *How I Got Away With It*.'

Right: Margot Fonteyn and Diana, who was a keen fund-raiser for Covent Garden.

Right: Alan Pryce-Jones, Diana, Hamish (Jamie) Hamilton, and Daphne Fielding, at the house of Patrick Kinross, one of the Neighbours.

Left: Diana and Noël Coward at Les Avants, his house near Montreux.

Below: Richard Bonynge, Vivian Cox, Graham Payn, Wendy Toye, Cole Lesley, Joan Sutherland, Noël Coward and Diana, on her last visit to Les Avants.

Right: Diana and Cecil Day Lewis at a party following the Duff Cooper Memorial Prize.

Above: Diana's grandson Jason at Schloss Prielau, the von Hofmannsthals' house in Austria.

*Above: Peveril and his mother
Lady John Manners, and Diana
with Doggie.*

*Opposite: Diana and Harold
Macmillan in the garden at
Haddon.*

*Left: Diana, Evangeline Bruce,
and Alastair Forbes at the
Haddon Ball, 1978.*

Opposite: With Harold Acton
in the garden of La Pietra,
Florence.

Above: Diana Phipps's Operatic Ball at Buscot, 1978. Left: Lord Goodman as Friar Lawrence, blessing Diana, dressed in her original Nun's costume from 'The Miracle', with Robert Heber Percy as Mephistopheles behind them. Right: with Lord Annan.

Opposite: With Nigel Ryan, at
Diana Phipps's house in
Tuscany.

Above: Patricia Hodge, who was to play Diana in 'Edward and Mrs Simpson', visiting the original at Warwick Avenue.

Left: Derek Hill.

Above: The Queen Mother greeting Diana.

Above: With Paul-Louis Weiller, the godfather of Artemis,
at her wedding to Antony Beevor, February 1986.

INDEX

Bold figures denote illustrations

LADY DIANA COOPER